AMÁ, YOUR STORY IS MINE

~

Amá,

YOUR STORY IS MINE

Walking Out of the Shadows of Abuse

~

BY ERCENIA "ALICE" CEDEÑO

Edited by Susan Dixon

UNIVERSITY OF TEXAS PRESS, AUSTIN

Requests for permission to reproduce material from this work should be sent to:
   Permissions
   University of Texas Press
   P.O. Box 7819
   Austin, TX 78713-7819
   www.utexas.edu/utpress/about/bpermission.html

∞ The paper used in this book meets the minimum requirements of ANSI/NISO
Z39.48-1992 (R1997) (Permanence of Paper).

Library of Congress Cataloging-in-Publication Data

Cedeño, Ercenia, 1949–
   Amá, your story is mine : walking out of the shadows of abuse / by Ercenia Cedeño ;
edited by Susan Dixon. — 1st ed.
      p.   cm.
   ISBN-13: 978-0-292-71656-8 (cl.: alk. paper)
   ISBN-10: 0-292-71656-7
   ISBN-13: 978-0-292-71657-5 (pbk. : alk. paper)
   ISBN-10: 0-292-71657-5
   1. Cedeño, Ercenia, 1949– 2. Cedeño, Ercenia, 1949—Family. 3. Mexican American
women—Biography. 4. Mexican American families. 5. Immigrants—United States—
Biography. 6. Mothers and daughters—United States—Biography. 7. Grandmothers—
United States—Biography. 8. Mexican American women—Social conditions—Case
studies. 9. Family violence—United States—Case studies. 10. Migrant labor—United
States—Case studies. I. Dixon, Susan. II. Title.

   E184.M5C383 2007
   305.868'720730092—DC22   2006037082
   [B]

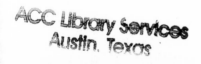

I dedicate this work to my brother, Joe. At the age of fourteen, you forfeited your dreams to support and protect your four little sisters. You took on the role of the man of the house to fill the void left by our father. Even at such a young age, you taught us the value of family, of commitment, of work, of honesty. I know that it was not easy to shepherd four strong-willed sisters, yet your protective arms were there for us as we huddled together, alone and fearful. No accolade is sufficient to thank you, Joe, for giving so much of yourself to us. Thank you, as well, for supporting my efforts to write our story from the moment I voiced my desire. Your affirmation has meant so much to me.

~

This book was written in honor of my Amá. She repeatedly told us as we were growing up that she was "sola una india," but she taught us values of one hundred years ago that endure today, and probably will for the next hundred years. Her strength and resiliency, and her commitment to those values, I now fully respect and appreciate. She remained true to her culture, refusing to adopt any superficial, passing trends of the day. She knew who she was and steadfastly held to her identity. To this day, her children continue to draw from the power of her beliefs, faith, and love.

CONTENTS

~

PREFACE

~

I sit next to my dying mother and I see her old, tired, soft face free of suffering and pain. I have so many thoughts and none of them makes sense. I am confused. I see my mother enjoying peace for the first time and I am not able to share that peace with her. I ask myself, "Will Amá really be happy now?"

We are all near her bedside in the hospital. One of my sisters is lying by Amá's side. Another one is throwing herself across Amá's body. The third is wailing and sobbing. My brother is stroking her hand. The demons of the past, like bats in a cave, have sat dormant in me for years, waiting to escape. But there I am, full of anger and bitterness, and, at the same time, numb. I wonder, "Am I so selfish and unforgiving that I can't feel the emotions my brother and sisters display?"

Why is it so hard for me to understand my mother, when she was so clear about who she was? Maybe it's because Amá talked in riddles. Many times I did not understand her. I spent most of my growing years mad at her and wanting her to change to fit in with the rest of the world. I thought of Amá as stubborn and narrow-minded. As we were growing up, my sisters and I tried to get her to change her way of dressing—always in conservative colors of navy blue, black, gray, and white, and always covering her soft and wavy hair. Her answer never varied: "You think that my clothes are going to change who I am inside?" When we wanted her to come and visit our friends' mothers, she would say, "Why do people need to know other peoples' lives?" And looking back, I wonder if she was really saying, "I don't want them to know our business." There was so much to hide. . . .

This is her story and, as it turns out, my own.

ACKNOWLEDGMENTS

I would like to acknowledge my son, José, and daughter, Debbie, who have motivated me all my life to grow. To all my dear friends who were patient with me during this time, thank you for the encouragement and faith you had in me, especially Marjorie Linder, Leola Momfrey, Alice Easley, Judy Wilson, Thais Thomas, Marian Moses, Gwen Kennedy, Patricia Thompson, Joan Jackson, Elaine Andrew, Diane Pleninger, Pat Kruse, and Marsha Graham. To my editor, Susan Dixon, I express my gratitude a million times over for her patience, honesty, knowledge, and expertise. Thank you for helping me to achieve the enormous goal of getting this work published.

Alice Cedeño's high school graduation, 1967.

Alice's sister Elisa at age fifteen with Amá at Lisa's "coming out" party, 1965.

Alice's sisters, Elisa and Estella, at Elisa's "coming out" party, 1965.

Joe and Estella at Estella's graduation from Calexico Union High School, 1968.

Elisa Rojas Torres, Amá, circa 1965.

Part One

~

Amá
~

As a young couple, Amá and my father, Apá, traveled through the United States in search of a new life. Nothing came easily for Amá. Even the weather was tough. She overcame blizzards, bitter winter cold, scorching sun, and typhoons. She faced many of life's deceptions by the early age of nineteen. By then her heart had already been broken by the loss of her first four *niños.* Amá experienced hunger, fear, humiliation, and injustice. Her beliefs were tested, but she hung onto them. She was like a tree that grew beside a river, offspring of the earth sustained by the waters of truth, whose roots were planted in good, firm, nourishing soil. With her heart rooted in this soil, she survived. Many times, looking withered and broken, she fooled you and came back even stronger.

Elisa Rojas Torres, my mother, was born in a small mountain village in northern Mexico. As my Amá would proudly say, "*Soy una india de la sierra.*" ("I am an Indian from the mountains.") She had no memory of her father, who died a year after she was born. I remember her telling us: "My mother tried to raise all three of us, but it became too hard. She found a nice man who was willing to marry her and keep us together. This, though, was not to be. Abuelito, 'Grandfather,' believed that only men of the same blood should share the same roof. Rather than giving my mother's new husband a chance, Abuelito parceled us out to different blood relatives. I was nine years old when Abuelito and Abuelita took me in. My sister, María, and brother, Felipe, were raised by my aunt."

Amá would often tell me of her life as a young child. "We had more important things to worry about than going to school. How could Abuelito have time to even think about sending us to school, when we had to work to survive each day? My sister and brother and I worked from dawn until dusk doing what we were trained to do. We worked the fields as soon as we were able to walk. My first chore, at early dawn, was to go check on my friends' animals and see if any of them had multiplied. I fed them and had them fat and ready to be sent to market. Others were served for dinner. At the age of nine, I could already outrun a chicken better than any adult could. I could twist its head off, clean it, and make fresh chicken soup. I could roast the red chiles until they danced on the *comal* and turn them with my bare fingers as easily as if they were tortillas.

"The scent of roasting chiles was so strong it would irritate the nostrils and throat, causing even adults to cry. Early in life, through the endurance of the burning noses and mouths, proud fathers would boast, 'Look at this girl—she'll be a real woman.' The more calluses and body scars, the prouder the fathers were. What I didn't know then, was that I was being taught how to be a good wife.

"Five years later, I was still sleeping with Abuelita, playing with dolls and reminiscing over the sweet stories of ancestors that had passed on to the other life. I was so familiar with the stories that I would finish them after Abuelita dozed off, looking more dead than alive. Many nights I questioned if she was still in her body. I threw my arm around her chest and felt if her heart was still beating. At that time, at fourteen, I wasn't a little girl nor yet an adult. I was, however, doing women's chores.

"Early in the morning I joined the other girls from the ranches on the long walk down to the river to get the wash done, with baskets of clothes balanced on our heads. The morning started with the fresh smell of earth, as the *abuelas* watered the ground to settle the dirt before starting the day. This day, as every day—the day I met your father—the sun was warming our backs, and the chickens and pigs were running in the front yard. The women were going around in circles, busily starting their day. We had done our wash, our dancing, and our dreaming in the river."

This was as far as Amá would usually get with her story about meeting Apá. When we asked what attracted her to Apá, she answered, with a sound of regret, "*Hijas*, you remember when you had your doll and you made her feel special? There were times when the baby doll just needed to be cuddled, kissed, and held close to your chest. Other times she was the ballerina that could fly, capturing the audience and taking their breath away. It was like that when I heard your father's voice. The happiest time with your father was just an illusion; it only lasted the lifetime of a rose. Why should I remember things? What could I know of love when I was fourteen?"

Amá's first encounter with Apá did begin like a fairy tale. After the girls finished the laundry, their reward was to bathe and play in the river. The brush and weed concealed the young women from anyone passing by. Wearing only their white cotton slips, they often danced with wild abandon. They did not realize that their slim, nearly naked forms were mirrored in the river like beautiful water lilies. Their voices were full of playful laughter. People passing by could hear the splashing water, but they respected the girls' modesty and continued on their way. Several times a week, Amá heard the voice of a young man singing as his horses trotted by. She was used to hearing this joyful voice and she would tell herself, "There is a man who loves his life and sings like a canary."

One warm afternoon, surrounded by a virgin land of untamed beauty, Amá felt safe and hidden from the outside world as she finished her basket of laundry. She slipped out of her dress and was wearing only her delicate white slip that was soaking wet from the healing, rippling water. Strolling among the yucca with its beautiful blossoms, she contemplated her life, hopes, and dreams. She marveled at the wonderful fruit-bearing cactus called *"su maguey"* while she spread her clothes out to dry on the spearlike leaves of the yucca. As she sat on ancient rocks to cool her feet, she observed the worn surface of the rocks, made smooth by countless generations of people passing by. She emerged from the reeds wearing her slip, feeling modest but unaware that the fragile, wet fabric simply graced her nudity.

Just as she was preparing to join the other girls in their bathing, she glanced up, sweeping back her waist-length hair, and was startled to find before her a young, dark man with a wide forehead. That should have been her first clue. Abuelita had warned her that people with wide foreheads were stubborn, but she forgot the warning the instant she saw the inviting smile in his eyes. Gallantly, he removed the sombrero that covered his coal black, curly hair. His eyes were intriguing— the dark shade of black olives. His hands were rough with calluses, showing that he was a man who earned satisfaction from his labor. Abuelita had told her, "If you want to really know a man, look at his hands and feet."

It was he whose voice had raised so much curiosity over the months. Several times a week he sang as he delivered meat from the family butcher. The two exchanged glances. They saw in each other's eyes their own beauty and desires. It was here that two worlds combined in a single moment of heaven on earth. Amá liked how open and unguarded he seemed. Apá was surely attracted by her shyness. He secretly followed her home and began tucking little notes for her in the cracks of the adobe bricks. As she found them, she would quickly hide them under her blouse, waiting until dark when her neighbor friend could read them to her.

Elisa was afraid to be discovered by her *abuelito*. She thought if she were found out, she would be sent away to live with an aunt in another town. Abuelito had noticed the attraction between the two youngsters and had warned her of the bad blood in Apá's family. Since only a hundred people lived in the village, the reputation of Apá's family was well known to all. His mother, the midwife Doña Demetria, was a woman who had broken all traditions. She smoked, drank liquor, and had numerous men in her life. She earned her name, *la mujer mala* ("the bad woman"). But in spite of these warnings, Amá responded to Apá's persistence. Eventually, with his whole tribe present, as called for by tradition, he asked for Amá's hand in marriage.

Apá had asked the village priest to the ranch to speak for him with Abuelito and to request Amá's hand in marriage. Juan, his oldest brother, came with Apá to stand in for the father they lacked. The men looked as if they had showered in dust. Apá and Tío Juan's white clothes were covered with dirt, and the priest's robe was not any cleaner. They all seemed tired, which seemed a strange sign, as they came down the dirt hill and approached Amá's *ranchito*. Flocks of people followed behind the priest, for any small event was big news. The ones who didn't join in would stretch their necks out their windows to see what was going on. The large *mamás* with their barefoot children, some bare-bottomed as well, followed the priest as if they were in a parade.

On that day, even the animals were on their guard. It was as if they knew something very special was going on. The chickens stayed in their corral, and the mules didn't follow their usual routine of mingling with the people.

The traditional, brightly colored bowls were scrubbed so

clean they looked brand-new. The wet earth smelled as clean as freshly bleached sheets. One could almost eat off the earthen floor, as it had been watered twice a day for the last week in order to keep the dust down.

When my Amá's *abuelito* saw Apá, his brother Juan, and the priest nearing the yard, he went out to meet them halfway. It would have been unusual for anyone to meet inside the house, as there was only one room, the bedroom, which was considered a sacred place that only family members could enter. Abuelito greeted the priest with the respect that was customary; he knelt and kissed his hands.

Without wasting any time, the priest spoke of the reason for his presence. He had come to ask for Elisa's hand in marriage, and he spoke of the intentions Apá had for her. Apá promised to take care of her, to be kind, considerate, loving, and loyal, and to build Amá her own home as soon as possible. He would be the kind of father he had always dreamed of having . . . one that would stick around. While the promises were being recited, Abuelito, with a glance, gave the order for María, Amá's sister, to bring refreshments. Each person was served warm cinnamon bread and a cup of hot chocolate, which had been made that morning with fresh cow's milk.

The spicy aroma brought to the young men's mind thoughts of the young girls who kneaded the soft dough every morning. In the pale light of morning, as they kneaded, the young girls' minds drifted from their work while they imagined a life far better than the ones they had. Their romantic illusions convinced them, at the age of twelve or thirteen, that the best part of life was belonging to a man.

The priest asked my mother to be present so he could hear her will, and Abuelito went to fetch her. Amá still wore her hair in two long braids falling to her waist and tied with wool strings. She was dressed in an apron that she herself had made, wrapped around her childlike body. She came forward shyly with her head down, as was expected when there were men around. The priest asked Amá if she was willing to become Fidencio's wife, and she solemnly nodded "yes." She knew that she was not to show any emotion or it would be interpreted that she was too *libre* ("anxious"). The priest announced that her answer was given and they would come back in five months to make sure that her answer was coming from her heart.

The five months was not an idle waiting period. During this time she had to learn what was expected of her in her husband's house, from scrubbing his pants on a rock by the river and making his underwear, to all the other duties of a wife.

At the end of the five months, they all met at the same place as before. Again the priest asked for Amá. Looking straight into her eyes, he asked, "*Hija*, do you have an answer for us?" She answered, "Yes, I will marry him." The priest asked her, "Is this of your own will?" Again she answered, "Yes."

"Now that you have given me your answer, I have a question," the priest said. The world became still and the neighbors fell silent and listened intently as he said, "Do you have anything to confess? Remember, you are not lying to me, you are lying to Mother Mary." Amá answered, "No, I have nothing to confess." Had Amá's virginity not been intact, she would have been returned to her family and the whole town would have turned their backs on her. But that would have been a gentler fate than the future she now faced with such naïveté.

It would take about a week to prepare the food for the wedding fiesta. But that was easy, for the uncles made their living by making *barbacoa* ("barbequing"). They came from a long line of butchers, so they expertly killed a couple of lambs, dug a hole in the ground, and cooked the meat. The aroma invited everyone to the fiesta. They brought with them gifts of live chickens, pigs, eggs, corn, and beans—whatever they had.

The women attended to the details of the wedding dress. One was in charge of the sleeves; another worked on the embroidered yoke. The lace, veil, everything was handmade. The gathering was a special time when the women came together to offer the young bride advice learned from their own experiences. My mother was petite, not strong and big like most women who worked the way she did. She was beautiful, with soft and supple skin, but her beauty was not an attribute that she wasted time with.

Her *tías* knew what was ahead of her. They accepted their duty of passing on the treasures of the wisdom, but they didn't understand that they were really conditioning her for the abuse that was to come. They said to her, "*Mi hija*, these are things that you have to know so that you don't learn the hard way. When a man sees you, he does not see a beautiful young lady. He sees a woman that he should own. He envisions himself with her in bed. A husband does not welcome these looks of lust. Avoid these men and their burning eyes. They scour you from head to toe. They make you feel as though you have undressed willingly for them. Keep your eyes lowered when you pass them—do not let them know that you see them. Cross your arms and walk quickly. Your husband will fault you for their behavior. Your beauty will be your burden. Men will take their anger out on their wives, cowards that they are. They learn *que el miedo no anda en burro* ("fear runs fast"). We know that there are husbands that don't even permit their wife to visit her own parents. If Fidencio is this kind of man, don't cross him; we will understand."

They told her if any man appears in her yard, to make sure she does not show her face unless her husband sends for her. She should never let any man inside the house, even her own uncle, brother, or *abuelito*. "Why?" Amá asked. "Just do what he says," they told her.

As Abuelita Angelita listened to their words, she knew Amá would become just a memory in their lives. She knew

Apá's family was hard-hearted and she would not be free to come and see them when her heart desired. Before the day of parting, Elisa spent many hours together with her sister, brother, and Abuelita, just brushing each other's hair. The love they shared would only come to life again in stories.

After the ceremony, Amá stayed one last night with her family, for she had just received the Holy Eucharist. It was considered sinful for her to consummate the marriage on this day. My father went home alone with Amá's dowry of a couple of pigs, handmade embroidered pillows and sheets, and a few crocheted doilies.

The next day at midmorning, Apá appeared on his horse. Standing in the yard was Amá's whole family. Her mother, sister, brother, aunts, and cousins were there to see her off. Doña Angel, Amá's mother, said, "Elisa, kneel down and receive your grandmother's benediction." Her *abuelita* crossed her shaking fingers to form a cross, blessed Amá's head, and said in a trembling voice, "*Qué Dios te bendiga y sea una buena esposa.*" ("May God bless you and may you be a good wife.") Abuelita, with a lump in her throat, stroked Amá's hair one last time, holding back tears she believed would bring Amá bad luck if they were spilled.

Apá boosted Amá onto the horse and threw two bundles up behind her. They rode away from the ranch, her family following them until they disappeared into the long rows of corn, leaving the rustling leaves and clouds of dust behind them. The farther away they got, they younger they seemed to be. The family hoped that Apá did not inherit the *alma negra de su madre* ("black nature of his mother").

Finally, Amá thought, she had a man to replace the one taken away from her in her youth, her father. She now had someone who would wrap his arms around her and call her his own. She had someone of her own as well, someone besides the doll with the cornhusk hair that she had cradled against her heart for so long. Looking back, Amá says, "I had no clue of what I was getting into. If only Abuelito had told me that this was the kind of hombre he used to tell stories of . . . hombres with the *diablo* inside of them. I would have been scared and more cautious, but instead I entered the marriage unprepared for the chaos of Apá's family. I thought I was going to my perfect home."

Instead, at the end of the horseback ride, what she discovered was a crazy mother-in-law who was more interested in a bottle of tequila and married men than she was in being a mother. Moreover, she found four brothers and three sisters in the home Apá brought her to. Amá was to share her dream home with four teenage boys who were no better than motherless untamed animals. She found that she had not only pledged herself to her husband, but to his family as well. Doña Demetria, Apá's mother, expected Amá to turn these animals into angels. She saw a mother for her children, not a daughter-in-law.

Amá cooked, cleaned, and tried to make sure that everything under her command was taken care of. When Doña was sober and her children could not be found to distribute the meat to vendors, she would wake Amá by grabbing her by the hair, demanding to know where they were. When Doña was drunk, she would come home with strange men and invite her children to drink with them. Doña Demetria was unable to control her wild children because they were doing exactly what she did. One of them had already been nearly killed for playing free with a married woman.

Amá was blamed for everything that went wrong. Doña Demetria beat her with a belt or broomstick, sometimes locking her in the outhouse while Doña rewarded my father with another woman. As the noise from their drunken party filled the night, Amá, a terrified child, faced her fear of what the coming darkness would bring. She learned quickly that for her to survive in this family, it was best to become invisible. She spent many nights crying, unable to escape when she heard the words of her mother-in-law, "Where is that woman?" When Doña came, Amá knew it was time to be beaten.

Amá had never been beaten by her own family. Nights had never been a source of terror as they were in this family. The dark had been a special time when her dear, gentle Abuelita would share with her the stories of their ancestors, passing on myths of graceful women. Now she prayed that she would just be left alone. She would prostrate herself to the Lord, begging him to give her a safe and loving home.

Instead, he gave Amá her firstborn child. Now she would have someone who would listen to her, someone she could talk to out loud and without fear. This baby would be like a bridge to another lifetime. She felt she no longer lived in vain.

Amá's favorite chore of the day was to go down to the river to wash the family clothing. She sat by the same rock every day, scrubbing the basketful of clothes while her mind wandered. She knew the name of her baby would be chosen by the religious calendar. Each day had a saint's name, and when a baby was born, it inherited that saint's name. Thereafter, the saint would be an advocate for this child for the rest of its life.

At home she would lie down on her straw mat. In the quiet of the hot, dark nights, she would hug her womb and, in a soft, secret voice, whisper her feelings for the life inside of her. She would profess her love to the little seed of life.

While Amá's stomach was secretly growing under her loose clothes, Apá wandered from ranch to ranch full of resentment and anger toward his mother. Even he could not understand the beatings he got from his mother. He would not return home until he had decided Doña was over her anger. Alone, Amá continued her exhausting chores from early morning until night. Now, she gave thanks for the darkness, for they would have her work nonstop like the animals if it were daytime.

As her time of delivery drew near the whole neighborhood anticipated this sacred event. Amá knew what was expected of her because she had been present at many other deliveries. As much as she feared Doña Demetria, she knew that her *suegra* knew her job well. No one talked about the coming birth, but there was a stillness that filled the house. Amá knew she had to be strong and endure her pain, for that was the nature of women. She knew, too, that she would get her little *comadrona*, which was made with two different kinds of tea with a shot of liquor. It was supposed to numb her pain. Doña Demetria claimed the potion would bring her contractions closer together. People trusted Doña with her herbs and traditional shaman rituals. They had no other choice, for there was no doctor in this village. If a woman suffered complications, she most likely would die, since it took four hours to get to the nearest town. There were no roads at this time, and the only way to travel was by donkey, mule, or cart. Amá prayed for a fast birth.

The mystery of birth was sacred. The family would gather to observe the miracle until the midwife, covered from head to toe in dark clothes, showed up with a pan of hot water in her hands and muslin cloth draped across her arm. The children would be sent outside with the husband, but even the youngest were aware of what was about to happen, for a baby would always appear. The villagers would continue their daily routines until the first cry of the child released everyone from the tension.

This was the only time Amá would be taken care of. She was nurtured by her *suegra* for thirty days in bed. Her head and feet were covered to keep her warm. She would not be allowed to stand up, so she was bathed in bed, and she was not allowed to leave the house. It was a time of prayer, at the end of which the baby was named and baptized.

The placenta and umbilical cord were considered sacred. Doña Demetria would carefully save them and place them on a big green leaf. She waited until midnight for the light of the moon, selected a small spot on the earth, dug a grave, and gently laid the placenta and umbilical cord to rest. The burial rituals were believed to assure that the newborn would return someday to his homeland. Some believed this determined the infant's fate in life.

While Amá carried her newborn son around in her shawl, Apá was struggling with his inner turmoil and rebellion. He struggled to be free of his family's expectations that he, too, would become a butcher. He chose to go to other ranches, each time going farther and farther away. Escaping the animosity he had for his family, he returned only infrequently. Again he impregnated Amá.

As she was nursing her second child, her firstborn son was withering away. He looked sicklier each day. As she held him close to her breast, he refused to nurse. Her lovely breasts were full to overflowing with nourishing milk. They were hard as pomegranates and ached constantly. She cried in pain, especially when she knew that her baby's mouth desperately searched for her breast even as he turned his head away from the life-giving nourishment. She knew that something was terribly wrong. At first she thought it was her milk, so she tried to make him his own *agua de arroz* ("rice water"). Still he refused to drink. The baby was dehydrated, burning away from the inside out. By the third day, he just lay like a rag doll. His eyes stared vacantly, looking like two small pieces of glass pasted to his face. Fever consumed his tiny body.

Doña Demetria wrapped him in mud to cool down the fever, but there was no change. His once pudgy hands were now just little bones, and his little face was only an outline of what it had been. Soon, his eyes could no longer open all the way. Doña prayed, sprinkled his body with holy water, and retried all her old remedies. Amá prayed and tried to bargain with God, lighting candles from morning to night. After fifteen days, he finally closed his eyes. His color had faded from healthy, living flesh to the pale blue of death.

The tiny child was buried wearing a little shroud made by his grandmother and a tiny scapular that once had been wrapped around his chubby neck. Now it hung loosely. Amá believed that Mother Mary would recognize and embrace this child buried with her own cloth.

Apá happened to be home at the time of the burial but only stayed a short time. He used the death of his son as yet another excuse to run away. He was there just long enough to impregnate Amá for the third time. Apá's visits were well tracked by Amá's stomach. Crying inside for her little lost baby, she was still able to give love and attention to her second *niño*. She soon began to notice this baby's life slipping away in the same manner as the first's. The cycle repeated itself.

Now, as she began to lose her second child, her once pleasurable trips to the river were repeated in torment. On her knees, with her arms outstretched as if she could see God and reach in his direction, she cried out, "Why is this happening to me? Why am I being punished? Why do you let me see their first smiles and hear them call me 'Mama'? Please don't give me any more babies if you are going to take them away!" She bowed her head, letting her tears join the river water, for she was about to bring her third baby into this world. Meanwhile, her second baby died.

The time of the *aguas* is the time of year that nature flourishes. Everything blooms and people nourish themselves from the crops produced during this time of plenty. Amá's third baby was thriving, looking healthy, fat and rich brown. Terrified by the past, she dropped to her knees to pound the ground with clenched fists. She pleaded to the mother of all Mexicans, and mother of all with Indian origins, la Virgen de Guadalupe, "You know the pain of being a mother. Please don't take this baby away." However, as the season ended and the fruit withered, so did Amá's third baby. He died just like the others.

Amá was not crying alone. Death was all around, brought

by an epidemic of scarlet fever. By now, Amá was eighteen years old. Forbidden to see her own family, she was unable to be comforted by her grandmother, the only person who truly cared for her. The only connection she had with her loved ones was an occasional tidbit of news passed on by a vendor who knew them. When her loneliness and the anguish of her losses overtook her and she allowed the pain to show, Doña Demetria would tell her, *"Tienes que aguantar. Tienes que ser mujer."* ("You have to put up with it. You must be a woman.") Doña would also ask her, "Why should you cry for something that has no solution?"

Within the next year, her fourth baby boy arrived. He lived past the sixteen-month danger point and Amá began feeling hopeful. Fooled by life, she began to do things she was unable to do before. She crocheted bigger booties and made little outfits for her healthy baby. Her joy, however, was short-lived. As he turned two, he became ill and eventually joined his three brothers. Another scar was added to her pierced heart.

Amá never let us forget our brothers. The only memento we had of these small seeds of life was a picture of one of the babies. That picture became a symbol of all four of them. Pointing to the picture of the baby with the dark, deep-set eyes and long, fanning eyelashes, the double chin and perfect little arms and fat legs, people would ask who the child was. We always answered, "He is our brother."

Escape to a New Life
~

No one ever left Rancho Salado. It seemed as impossible as touching the sky. In Amá's time people didn't have money to just leave when they wished. Yet, Amá could dream. Dream about a life somewhere else, somewhere else far away from her in-laws and the cursed ranch. Amá prayed to the little ones in heaven to help her change her life. She never imagined that her wish was but a step ahead. This night would be different.

Apá and Doña Demetria were both out on a drinking binge. Amá was left to look after her youngest brother-in-law. She never knew when to expect Apá back. Through the noise of rain pounding on the roof and water dropping outside into puddles, Amá heard a commotion. She grabbed her lantern to give enough light to see her way to the door.

In burst Apá, breathing hard, as exhausted as a runner finishing a marathon. He was frantically spitting out words, *"¡Elisa, me vienen siguiendo y me quieren matar!"* ("Elisa, they are after me and they want to kill me!") He knew nobody ever lived to talk about it after being caught in bed with another man's wife.

No sooner had Apá finished talking than the thundering hoofbeats of galloping horses filled the night air. For a second Amá thought they were going to tear through the door. Apá shouted, "Elisa, tell them I am not here!" When the men pounded on the door, Amá got close to the door and said, "Is that you, Fidencio?" Hearing this, the men thought their wanted man hadn't made it home yet, so they left in a hurry.

Frightened, broke, and with no destination in mind, Amá and Apá escaped that night to start a new life. My mother thought, "Now we are free," never realizing Apá was her curse.

While traveling on their journey on primitive roads, sometimes in buses and other times on foot, they would stop for a short time to work on ranches. Sometimes they just earned their food for the day. Other times they were paid with what they helped grow or harvest. But Apá was a devil of a barterer and would find a way to turn goods into change.

The young couple continued to work their way from one ranch to the next with the intention of getting closer to the North. Amá would tell us later about the times that she was almost ready to give up. She grew so tired of living in the huts and shacks, being treated like animals by the rancheros. Undernourished and underpaid, almost destitute, they carried on, working the corn, bean, and cotton fields. That was when Amá found out Joe was on the way.

Again with child, Amá knew she had to continue on. She must survive for this baby. The months and days passed by, and Joe was born as they traveled through a *pueblito* called Salines, Mexico. They didn't plant any roots, and their pesos seemed to disappear almost before they were earned. Amá spoke later of the days they went without eating at all. They spent only what was necessary for Joe to survive. They were saving the pesos needed to cross the river to the land in the north where everything came easy and money grew on trees.

Finally, they reached Torreón, Coahuila. It was not long before Apá became familiar with the town and made some friends. He felt comfortable and safe leaving Amá and Joe behind while he went to try his luck across the river and to make money for the *enganche* (the "contact man").

Amá didn't hear from Apá for several months. She was frightened, at all times expecting the worst. She thought he had left her, as he was accustomed to doing in his other relationships. This time Amá was wrong. One day Apá appeared very mysteriously in the front yard, where Amá happened to be doing her washing. Apá had arrived to arrange with another man their crossing over the river. Amá was advised to not carry anything except her child in one arm and a light parcel in the other. They instructed her to be prepared to run in any direction if necessary. Amá did as she was told, leaving everything behind, even her wedding treasures.

Their mission began on foot early one summer dawn. This was to be a new beginning, one of many to come. They met with the Coyote. The Coyote, with his Texas boots and khaki pants, herded them along gruffly. His attitude was like that of a cheap drug dealer. They moved through the heat of the summer sun for miles across the desert, becoming increasingly sunburned and dehydrated. During the dark, moonless night the point of connection was to be reached. Even the common sounds of mosquitoes buzzing, frogs croaking, crickets chirping, and woodpeckers pecking created panic. The silent armadillo, slithering through the cactus, sent goose bumps of fear up and down their skin.

They breathed a deep sigh of relief when they saw the six other uncertain and scared shadows sitting on the ground. Here were others, hugging their knees, waiting for the moment to cross the river to a better life. The agreement with the contact man was made and paid for ahead of time so that a place would be saved for them. The river was low and the night was calm. This would have been in their favor had the Coyote been honest. But now he had their money. He took them in a canoe to the opposite side of the Río Bravo, and when they stepped out on the shore, they turned to find that he had deserted them and was heading back in the opposite direction, breaking his promise to lead them to shelter.

Shocked and abandoned, they hauled their dripping, wet bodies to the shelter of some brush under the orange trees. Camouflaged by the underbrush, they cupped their hands over Joe's mouth so he would not cry out and draw la Migra ("the immigration agents on patrol").

The next portion of the journey was through a dangerous combat zone. They had to avoid being detected at all costs. All the horror stories they had ever heard raced through their heads. La Migra entertained themselves by making cruel exhibitions of the refugees they caught. People had been beaten and dragged for miles for the amusement of la Migra. At the end of an entire day of desperate fear, they reached the nearest Texas town.

Apá went into town to try to find someone he could trust, someone who spoke his own language and would give him a helping hand. As Apá walked away, he heard Amá praying to the Virgen de San Juan de los Lagos to keep him from harm. He turned to look at his wife, and it seemed as if the saint she was speaking to was standing right in front of her, so intense was her faith.

Amá tried to hide. She did not want to be noticed in her rebozo, or shawl, which was now so dirty from groveling on the ground and under bushes. It seemed she was so dark in this crowd of whites. Fortunately for them, Apá found one of his own people, who took them to a rusty, boarded-up barn. What was left of the barn that wasn't sinking into the ground was still being used to shelter people from many different Mexican states, all of them searching for the easy dollars. Amá had to steel herself against the stench of this barn, not fully realizing that it was there she would have to spend the night.

As the day came to an end, Amá saw the men, women, and children lying mixed together in a disorderly mass. Strangers were breathing on each other's faces, rubbing body-to-body, infants and adults. This was repulsive to her, reminding her of pigs wallowing together in the mud back home. This situation she would not accept, so she took Joe and her one blanket and unrolled it outside. She hadn't lived in such a filthy pigsty in her own country, and she would not here, either. She fell asleep and woke to the freshness of the morning with Apá by her side.

That morning Apá followed some of the men who had heard that there was a truck on the way to pick up migrant workers. He wanted to determine if there was any danger of being checked for green cards. While Apá was gone, Amá waited anxiously, knowing he might be caught at any moment. Amá played her luck, too. She knew that if she wanted to get work, she would have to look for it herself.

Tired of waiting, she grabbed Joe and walked out of the sheltering barn, observing carefully so she would know her way back. She passed by a few ranches, but one with a yellow house drew her. Perhaps it was the alluring smell of frying bacon that touched her hungry stomach, or the sensuous aroma of freshly baked bread. Maybe it was the love and respect that Amá had for any living and growing thing, as trees surrounded the ranch, with wildflowers growing like untouched gifts from nature. The white and yellow daisies growing all around announced their freedom to her.

There was quite a bit of activity in this place, she guessed, from the tractors, tillers, and stacks of crates piled high in the barn. Amá cautiously approached the back door, hoping to catch a glimpse of the woman of the house. Instead a white man appeared inside the screen door. Terrified, she heard the door squeak open, but then she heard a kind voice speaking to her. She could not understand his English, but she sensed he was asking her what she wanted, so in her own invented sign language, she pantomimed what she could do: wash, mop, scrub, iron, and so on. The man looked at her and at Joe and nodded. She could stay and work. She thanked him over and over.

As the days passed, Apá would go to meet Amá at the ranch, and they would walk back to the barn together. While he waited for Amá to finish her work, he might fix something he noticed needed mending. Soon the owner observed Apá's desire to work, and he was hired also. It was only a few days after they had both been working there that the owner asked if all three would like to come and live in a little room off the kitchen.

For the first time, Amá discovered that, besides her blood family, there were other people, too, who were kind, and there was another way of life full of love and comfort and good health for those who shared it. The kind American lady made her feel accepted and comfortable. Soon they were sharing recipes, and my mother was teaching the lady to make tortillas from scratch. In return, she taught Amá to use the washing machine and other marvels of the household. Since Amá had always distrusted doctors and their medicine, she planted an herb garden and shared with the lady the ancient arts of healing.

As for Joe, he was able to enjoy life as a little boy. He had the whole ranch to explore, and he ran back and forth in the sunshine, smelling the new-mown hay and talking to the big brown-and-white cows. Often he would wave to the truck drivers who sped by on their way to the big city. He also made a loyal friend of Charlie, a collie who stayed by his side all day and slept with him at night.

The more comfortable their life became, the less fearful of the law my *apá* became. He started going back to his old ways, spending his nights at the cantina, bragging and dreaming about what life could be rather than what it really was. Apá's spirit got lost in the search, and he never took the time to ask himself what he was seeking. Amá, hopeful and devoted, thought it was an expression of his youth and that he would one day mature. This meant that she would continue to do what he asked.

One day he told her to pack up their few possessions and get ready to leave. At midnight they slipped into the night, dragging the sleepy Joe. The dog understood that he was leaving. He tugged on Joe's pants. Apá comforted Joe with a lie, "Don't worry. We'll come back someday for the dog." With that, they entered the darkness.

La Migra

Apá felt like a king, full of ideas and power. Unfortunately, his subjects were just like himself, no power and no papers. Now they, too, were a part of the legions jumping on the backs of flatbed trucks. The Mexican contractor, forgetting his own roots, treated them all like animals, shoving them into the truck and calling them burros. Then it was on to McCullough, Corpus Christi, to Colorado and Montana, always running and full of fear. They sometimes saw the camps being raided by la Migra, but somehow they always escaped.

The migrant workers moved regularly as the agents got closer, leaving behind their pay. Their meager possessions became fewer and fewer with each move. They were always just a step ahead of the long arm of la Migra. Somehow, though, in spite of all this, Apá felt he would never be caught, and even sent for his brothers from Mexico. One of Amá's worst nightmares soon became a reality. She would again suffer at the hands of her in-laws.

Apá carried out his schemes without Amá's knowledge. She was left to work in the fields, keeping Joe by her side. Much to her dismay, when she returned from the fields one day, she saw Apá standing with two couples who looked like they had just come across the river. They were two of his brothers and their wives. Amá was so shocked she felt the blood going up and down her body. Not daring to express her feelings, she swallowed her anger and followed Apá's direction to "find a place for them to crowd in." The next day they found work and fit right in with the other migrants because they knew how to work the crops.

However, the brothers couldn't adjust as Apá had to the undercover nature of the work. In the Forties, Americans felt threatened by the infiltration of Mexicans. They wanted the cheap labor and energy the migrant workers provided, but they also wanted these people to vanish back across the border. Often the workers were denied access to stores, restaurants, and water fountains. They were viewed in the towns as tramps, subjected to catcalls and hurled obscenities everywhere they went. Amá said that it didn't hurt much, that they were just *gente sin corazón* ("people with no heart"). What did scar her heart was what she put Joe through during the months of migration with his uncles.

Nightly gatherings began with a feeling of relief that the working day was over, but that soon was followed by the drinking of a great deal of mezcal. Recalling the grudges of bygone years, the men proceeded to fight, to show each other what a real hombre was. When they were finished, they began the abuse of their wives.

But Amá had another terror. Young Joe was jerked from her side as they walked into the drunken circle of men. His face showed no sign of fear or weakness. His uncles whipped him and shouted at him, "Only *vergas* cry!" My mother placed herself between them to keep Joe from being beaten, but they pushed her out of the way, taunting her, "Do you want him to grow up to be a sissy?" Distraught, Amá begged in a harsh whisper, "*¿Dios mío, por qué mejor, no me quitas la vida de una vez?*" ("My God, why don't you take my life right now?")

Apá's brothers didn't last long, though. They failed to adapt to the ways of migrant workers—they had no experience walking with their faces downcast, never looking an American in the eye. They made spectacles of themselves on the street, were arrested and shipped back to Mexico. They never returned.

Three weeks before their capture, the camp was raided while Apá, Joe, and the *tíos* were picking oranges three miles away. Amá had stayed behind to prepare dinner. The families were gathering for the evening meal. The smell of carne and tortillas drifted in the air. Some of the men were in the showers, and women were breastfeeding their newborn babies. Others had gone to the water ditch to wash their clothes. Suddenly the piercing sound of a whistle and screeching of tires filled the air, and a cloud of dust arose in the camp. The people were in terror as the immigration agents roughly hauled them off in trucks to the detention center.

Apá returned with a basket of oranges to a scene that was like a battleground after an invasion. Left behind were the baby bottles, rebozos, saints' statues—all their most intimate treasures. Gone were the Mexican wool blankets that had marked each family's territory. The fear of those taken hung in the air, along with their cries. Apá just stood there, anger rising as he viewed the devastation. The pulse throbbed in his temples.

Joe frantically stormed around calling, "Amá! Amá! Amá!" hoping the air would carry his voice to her. He ran in search of Amá, with Apá following. He looked for her in all of the places he and Amá spent time together. Apá spotted a box in the shade of a tree. The box was moving. It started to rise up and pretty soon two feet appeared underneath the box. It was Amá!

Apá and Amá traveled back and forth, following the crop seasons from Montana to Colorado. In the first days of a beautiful, clear July, a voice without words can be heard to say, "Live, grow, flower!" The people sing without a reason and flowers spring from the earth. The ground returns a perfect crop in exchange for the many hours it is cultivated by hundreds of hands that depend on it to keep their own seeds of life growing. It was in such a time and place that my sister Mary was born.

For Joe, the day went on as usual—people going about their business, men shaving, women combing their children's tangled hair, the bus driver washing the bus for the next day. What wasn't normal was that Apá wouldn't let him into the shack to see Amá. Instead, there were two ancient women with faces of stone, bodies of steel, and the eyes of tigers. Their movements were swift and deliberate. Their outward appearance suggested that they were mute and had shut out the world, yet they controlled everything with their eyes. They had become midwives based on their maternal instincts. Only they were allowed in and out of the shack.

Daylight was about gone when Apá started a bonfire. He still wouldn't let Joe see his *amá.* Finally, one of the two old women came out and asked Apá for a pot of hot water. Moments later, with a shrill, newborn cry, Mary entered the scene. From then on, Mary became a part of her brother. He learned to know her needs by her different cries. Her face was not the face of an infant. Her high cheekbones and deep, black eyes with their prominent eyebrows revealed the role she was to play in life; she was to be a leader of the family.

By the time they finished the crop season, Apá had become increasingly homesick for his Mexican home and family. It seemed to him that the dream they came to America to chase was always pushed out of reach. Apá had grown weary of pursuing it. He and some other families who felt repressed by the U.S. government's rules and restrictions turned themselves in to the immigration authorities so they would be shipped to the nearest border. Apá always said, "Here in America the government tells you what to do. In Mexico I'm my own boss. I tell people what to do."

So it was back to Mexico, and back to the male freedom

Apá desired. Back to the three-room adobe house, the unpaved streets with wash hanging out in every yard, where it was not uncommon for three families to live together. The men didn't seem to notice the crowding. They left their houses at midmorning with full stomachs and returned only to sleep after long, lazy hours spent prowling the streets, drinking, laughing, feasting, and being completely free of any moral constraints.

It was more difficult for the women, who had no room to create the comfort they had enjoyed in America. Amá missed the privacy of her own family circle, not to mention the conveniences of a stove, running water, and electricity. In the pueblo the electricity consisted of one wire that ran from the neighbor's house to theirs, and this was only if the neighbor was willing to allow them to share his bill. They were entitled to only one light bulb, which had to be placed in the kitchen, where so much of the women's work was performed.

As for plumbing, the streets were always torn up, as if the pipes were being installed, giving them the look of a permanent war zone. But the running water never came.

Again Amá had the fear of bacteria in the milk, water, cheeses, and vegetables. Everything she fed her family needed to be boiled. There was no icebox available, and food was left out day and night, with the possibility of spoilage. If it tasted a little strange, Joe did not complain. If he did, it meant Amá had to stand in line to reuse the community stove to recook the food; it could not be wasted or thrown away.

It wasn't even a month after the family had returned to Mexico that Mary's pudgy face began to wither with dehydration. Apá was terrified that Mary, his pride and joy, would end up like the dehydrated dogs that withered away in the streets. Her illness changed the direction of their lives. When they returned to Texas to save Mary, Apá and Amá put their children's lives on a different path. Though their Mexican heritage would remain, they would become Americans.

Amá always blamed fate for the way her life turned out. Perhaps this kept her from becoming bitter. Work and duties consumed every day of Amá's life. She often felt like a cripple, yet she seemed a tower of strength. A husband assured her a place in the community, safe from wagging tongues. It was believed that a woman who had children and no husband in the household was unfit, and her daughters would grow up to be prostitutes. Amá wanted to believe her marriage was like a tandem bicycle, but in reality, she was riding it by herself.

To the outside world Apá presented a perpetual, contented smile. To his family, his countenance could carry the sudden destructiveness of a bolt of lightning, devastating its target. Amá could never go forward with Apá. He was like an unexpected accumulation of rumbling, black thunderclouds of misery. As soon as Amá settled down to make a home for us, he inevitably wanted to move on to another place. He saw no need for Amá to have her own place, her own things. Apá never noticed that our *amá*'s greatest deprivations were security and rest.

Once Mary's health improved, Apá and Amá resumed the standard migrant workers' run from Texas to Colorado, then north to Montana, where their biggest fear was realized. It was one of those cloudy and misty evenings where the clouds were so low that you could almost touch them. Apá had just come in from work, leaving his boots outside the door. His chest was bare and his belt unbuckled, as he was changing out of his dirty clothes. Amá was getting dinner. Joe was on the floor playing with Mary when there was a knock on the door. Apá opened the door thinking it was his boss, the *patrón*, with forgotten work plans for the next day. Instead it was two men dressed in green, complete with brass buttons and a badge with a picture on their chests. The men marched their way in, asserting their authority and superiority by intimidating and terrifying the young family as they flashed immigration badges in front of Apá's face. Amá gathered baby Mary and Joe, and the three huddled at the end of the bed, holding on to the flowered curtain that partitioned the kitchen from the sleeping area as if this would protect them.

One officer sternly questioned Apá, asking him how he got to the United States and how long he had been in the country. The other officer looked around. Mary began to gurgle and coo, and he couldn't resist the temptation to go pet her. Mary batted her long, dark eyelashes at the officer and charmed him with her smile. Then this officer, in broken Spanish and hand gestures, asked Amá where Mary had been born. Amá answered, "In Colorado, Señor."

The man excused himself, walked to his partner, and mumbled that he needed to talk to him outside. Reentering the house, they asked Apá if he could call the ranch owner over so they could talk to him. Apá hurried and brought him over. They questioned him about what kind of people they were, to which he answered, "They are loyal, responsible, and very dependable. Mr. Fidencio and his family are part of our family." The officer asked, "So you would not mind writing a letter promising them work year-round?" "That is not a problem," el Ranchero replied.

The following Monday Apá and Amá went to the immigration office. Mary's birth in the United States gave them the right to become citizens. Once again, her influence determined the family's destiny. Within a month they had the papers that would free them from their life as fugitives.

El Ranchero liked Apá and Amá's work, and wanted us to stay on after the harvest season. The owner offered Apá a job winterizing the farm. He tried staying there longer than usual, but as the days began getting dark earlier he could feel the signs of the bitter winter on its way. Apá found the stillness and solitude suffocating. He decided he would not be able to tolerate the long winter days, looking like nights, the season seeming to last forever. He longed for his native environment. There was nothing left that he could identify himself with:

no other seasonal workers around, no amigos he could run off with. He felt like a stranger within his own family because he had been away from them so much.

Apá decided to leave. He had had enough of the dry, dusty chaff-laden wind to clog his lungs for a lifetime. The few shops in town were closed by the time his sixteen-hour day ended. He had saved quite a bit of money since there was nowhere to spend it. He was tired of this one-horse town and living his life according to a cow's schedule. He set his sights on Salinas, California.

Amá, on the other hand, was upset about leaving her friends of three seasons. Their lives had grown together like the roots under that dry Montana soil. She was devastated because she had acquired her own things, like the kitchen table Apá had made and all the kitchen utensils she needed. The little added-on room they lived in was the closest she had ever come to having her own home. Apá promised that in Salinas the children would be allowed to go to school; in Montana he had said there was no time to waste on it.

Apá had heard great things about Salinas—promises of jobs that would last the whole year long, and stories that all Mexicans were well received. He wooed Amá with his own promises and commitments. . . . If they both worked hard and saved, they would buy a house.

With more money in his pocket and his green card, Apá developed a sense of status. The family boarded the train, hopeful that life was going to be different. After a long day and night on the train, they arrived in Salinas. Apá told them to wait at the train station, just for a while. He would soon return. Lunchtime came, people came and went. Mary grew fussier and fussier as Joe walked her in and out of the station, trying to keep her entertained. Dinnertime passed, and there was still no sign of Apá.

The station closed at ten o'clock, and one old attendant in khaki work pants was the only person left besides them. He tried to mind his own business, smoking his cigar and pushing his broom, gathering up coffee cups and cigarette butts, and sweeping up heaps of dirt. Once in a while he looked at them through spectacles that dropped down to the tip of his nose. Finally, his broom came closer and closer to where they sat. He cleared his throat and asked Amá if there was anyone he could call to come pick them up.

Amá answered, "No, my husband should be on the way." At ten, he approached again and told them he was sorry but he had to close the doors. Turning to Joe, Amá said, "Come on, son, pick up your sister. We must wait outside now." She gathered up her bundles and took her children out into the night. The three huddled together on a bench, frightened and worried about what the night would bring.

Strange sounds filled the darkness: the snoring of drunks sleeping against the station wall, beggars rattling the garbage cans to find food, like hungry raccoons trying to fill their bellies. Amá and Joe, weary from their travels, fought off sleep for fear they might be attacked. "Don't despair. The Virgin Mary is going to help us," she encouraged Joe. Finally, in the middle of the night, Amá's faith was rewarded. Two flashing headlights of a car approached. Two shadows climbed out of the car. One was Apá, beaming with success and good news. He had made a friend who arranged for an apartment and would drive us to our new home.

Amá forgot her fatigue when she stepped into the yard. Apá had indeed been lucky. They had the honor of a house in a neighborhood where the families even had their names printed on the mailboxes. Here the families had already paid their dues, and had worked themselves up from toiling on the land to operating the packing machines. These people worked in the canneries, wearing white uniforms, white hairnets, and plastic gloves to protect their hands. Although many complained of rheumatism coming from the long hours their feet were soaked in the cold water that overflowed from clogged pipes, they at least enjoyed the luxury of stable hours. The outside of their houses showed this stability. Little blue houses with tiny porches and massive hanging flower baskets lined the street. Fences of roses separated the houses. Along the curb there was even a 1940s-vintage car, the chrome polished to perfection.

Amá breathed deeply the aromas of her new home. She walked over to the kitchen window and peered through. She stood there dazed, soaking in the experience. She thought to herself, "My past is finally gone." She toured the rooms, looking at the faded linoleum, with some wear spots peeking through. The rooms were vacant, closets exposed to the world without their doors. She walked royally through her new castle. She would call this home. Life would be good from here on, she thought.

Apá bought a used car. Work was good for them both in Salinas. Joe had never been so happy now that he was attending school. Amá hauled Mary to work with her every day in the fields. The first years of Mary's life were spent out in nature. She was used to thunder, rain, dirt, and noise. Noises of the trucks were common sounds of the day for her, making it easy for Amá to work all day. Two years later, Estella was born. All the while, Amá was pinching and saving her money with the goal of buying a house. But while Amá saved, Apá was spending more and more money and time away from home, cruising the cantinas with his compadres. The hell began again: violent outbursts, Amá's sobbing voice in the night, followed by Mary's crying and baby Estella's screams. Amá's dreams of security turned into a nightmare. Again she had to hide her bruised and swollen face, and lie to cover up the truth.

Apá began pulling Joe out of school three months out of the year to go work in Corcoran to pick cotton. By missing so much school, he was always the oldest in the classroom. In the third grade he was eleven years old. If it were not for truant officers hunting him down and forcing Apá to put him in school, he probably would not have gone at all.

When the officer asked Apá if he was sending Joe to school in Corcoran, he answered, "Yes." Then the man turned to Joe and asked him if he was going to school there. "No," he answered defiantly. Apá was furious that his son didn't follow his lie, making him look bad in front of the officer. "Apá, it's very easy for them to find out the truth; all they have to do is make a phone call and you'll get in more trouble." His father didn't even wait for him to finish before turning his back on him and walking away.

Slowly life was changing. They seemed to fit into the new neighborhood. More and more, Apá would come home and spend time with the family. Amá was pinching and saving money with the goal of buying a home. The family was getting used to a routine and having stability, but unfortunately that didn't last long. It lasted just long enough for Apá to find his group of amigos.

Joe Recalls
~

Joe and I sit in the Los Angeles hospital, sharing the last hours of our mother's life. A respirator keeps her body with us, though we know her spirit has slipped away. Suddenly all the suppressed emotions of a lifetime surge from her son, and he exclaims to no one but himself, "*Mi mamacita* finally got to the end of the road!" Choking back tears, his fists clenched, he struggles to gain control.

"*China*," he asks me, "do you want to know about the day you were born?"

"Yes, Joe, I want to know. What happened?"

"I remember a very clear night. The breeze was just right, the trees were full of color, and the night train to Los Angeles had already passed, shaking the house on its foundation. Now all was quiet. We had all gone to bed, Amá staying up late as usual. She always got up before anyone else, starting ahead of the day, but this morning I knew something was different because she wasn't up and making her usual sounds of pots and pans, running water, or footsteps rushing about. Then I heard Apá threaten to hit her if she didn't get up. I tiptoed toward their room, to peek in and see what was wrong."

"Don't cry, Joe. Tell me the story later."

"No, let me finish. I heard Amá say, '*Por favor, Fidencio, déjame quedarme en la casa.*' ('Please, Fidencio, let me stay home today.') I knew now that something was definitely wrong. Nothing stopped Amá from going to work. I had seen her work through fevers, black eyes, bruises on her shoulders. And now she refused to get up. Apá grabbed her by the hair and demanded she get out of bed. She rose and dressed slowly, unable to even bend over and tie her own shoes. I offered to help her but Apá threw me out of the way. I saw her get in the car and leave. I went to school, but all I could think of that day was Amá looking like she was in so much pain.

"After school I waited anxiously for them to come home. Five o'clock arrived and there was no sign of them. At eight, I heard the car drive up. I ran out and found only Apá. Oh, no, I thought, what has he done to her? I learned then that after working all day, Amá had had to be rushed to the hospital. En route, they were pulled over for speeding. The policeman who stopped them assisted in your birth. Your name was given to you by a nurse who suggested a number of names to Amá.

She didn't understand what she was being asked to do, to name the child, but the nurse took Amá's smile to mean a choice."

I felt my heart gallop in my chest. Could I have inherited Amá's pain and anger from when I was in the womb? I said to Joe, "I have always thought that I was born angry. Maybe we should let the past sleep. Now I am the one who is crying. Talking about the past is too much like reliving it in the present."

"It was a hard time right after you were born," Joe continued. "You contracted rheumatic fever and had temporary palsy for more than a year. To make matters worse, Lisa was born prematurely a year and a half later. Amá struggled with both of you. Lisa needed extra care and had to stay in the hospital longer. Amá couldn't do it all because she still had to bring in a paycheck. It couldn't have been done without the neighbors' help, taking you to doctor's appointments, seeing that the medicine was given on time, feeding us. Seeing Amá so overwhelmed with responsibility, they even offered to adopt you two.

"One afternoon your godmother, Doña Teresita, was tired of seeing Amá on her knees, bent over the sink, perpetually washing loads of diapers and never able to catch up. She thought she was being a Good Samaritan and suggested a washing machine to ease Amá's burden. Amá hesitated for a moment, thinking of Apá, but Teresita offered to let Amá use her credit at the store.

"When Apá came home at midnight from his outing and saw the washing machine, he became furious. He woke Amá and demanded the money she had saved for the home they were to buy one day. I pleaded in silence for her to do it, and she bent down to the bottom drawer, moved some canned goods, pulled out her jam jar full of money, and handed it to him. I thought for sure he was going to leave right there and then, but he didn't. The next morning he still remembered the money and claimed he was going to either find a house or put the money in the bank. But he didn't come back. And Amá was sick with worry, afraid some tragedy had happened to him."

Joe smiled wryly as he continued, "We didn't hear from him for weeks. In fact, that same weekend he was picked up by the border patrol for trying to smuggle prostitutes into the United States. Apá's immigration papers and right to stay in the country were taken away.

"While this was going on, Estella was three years old and quick and sharp, which often ended in disaster. She got hold of some matches and started a fire in the house. We were unable to save any of our belongings; all that was left of the house was rubble. Again the neighbors came to our rescue. The landlady gave up her garage to provide us a new start. These were days of great hardship for all of us. I learned to take care of the bills when I was twelve. I took care of you girls after I got home from school. Your Teresita helped with whatever I didn't know how to do. But regardless of the hard times, we were happy because, finally, our *apá* wasn't around hitting Amá."

Mexicali

~

As we began to adjust and learn to enjoy life without fear, our father decided to repent and fulfill his duties as a husband and father. He contacted Amá from Mexicali, a city just across the border in Mexico, by way of the neighbors' telephone, or sent letters with people who came our way. He persisted every way he could, until he got to Amá's heart again by promising to build a house. He told her that the Mexican government was making it very easy to purchase land, and that we now owned a piece of land, but he would not build if he didn't have his family with him.

Our neighbors, Teresita and Timo Marquez, warned Amá about Apá's sweet-talking and his false promises. They told her that Mexicali was *peor que un infierno* ("worse than hell"). They encouraged her to stay in Salinas for her children's sakes, telling her she would soon be getting a job in the canneries. Teresita and Timo reminded my mother how Apá's mother, the hateful Doña Demetria, had mistreated her. They told her that her hateful brothers-in-law were also now living in Mexicali. But she turned a deaf ear.

Once again we were on the road with another neighbor, Dino Roberto, driving us to Mexicali. Amá did absorb some of the advice she was given by the Marquezes, such as renting a room on the U.S. side of the border, so we could have an address to prove we were residents of the United States, and so Mary and the rest of us could attend school.

We crossed the Mexican border, and the first block was full of vendors slapping wares in front of the tourists' faces, blocking their view. It might have been a pair of sandals or a *pan dulce* ("sweet roll"). Darting children hung onto people's shorts, one offering his *chicles* ("gum") and another begging for a dollar, both at the same time. There were men offering the deal of the day: colorful wool serapes. The crazy taxi drivers wouldn't take no for an answer and followed so closely that it was impossible to get away from them. Confused and lost, people were running into one another, not knowing when to cross the street. The lights meant one thing to the pedestrians, another to the drivers.

In spite of all this, we were drawn like small magnets to our

Apá's eyes when we saw his smiling face. Don Roberto stopped the car and we all jumped out. It felt like we were all one again. We pulled Apá into the car and sat on top of one another to make room for him. Don Roberto drove us into many different neighborhoods where the houses had no numbers; the streets were narrow and full of holes. We drove on to the outskirts of town and down to the end of the road to old, open cotton fields, where Apá said, "We're here." Don Roberto rolled the big black 1940 Ford to a stop in front of a cardboard shack that looked so tiny in the middle of the abandoned, parched cotton fields.

There was old energy deposited into the sandy cracks and dry, white soil. As we started walking along the small path my father had made, chills ran all over my body, followed by the thought that these fields belonged to the past. It felt as if ghost relatives were revisiting, hovering and sobbing over the desolate fields as they saw the ruins that were left. The solitary plants had old wisps of cotton clinging to the withered, shriveled stalks. Without a bit of wind blowing, there were times that the wisps trembled, as if a ghost had passed by, leaving a silent cry of agony behind. It seemed this was the place where little children had scampered ahead of their *amás*, as adults pricked their bleeding fingers raw with the cotton thistles. Their shoulder blades were worn to the bone by the enormous, hundred-pound sacks they dragged from field to field.

As we got to the heart of the fields, we saw what appeared to be long-term campers without a camp. There were families living in tents made of sheets, others under a cardboard roof, and others who just spread a blanket for the night. Everyone was working toward the same goal—a home. This bonded them all together. They shared with each other what little they had. The pots and pans rotated from block to block. Someone's smell was everyone's smell. A conversation had many listeners. The mosquitoes didn't discriminate; they bothered us all in the same way. Everyone reprimanded everyone else's kids. The snoring men sounded like bears waking up after hibernation. That was a good way of scaring away the hundreds of fleas. We all shared the same light, the same sun.

Our house was one of the first to be built. It was because of Amá working long hours that we had the house at all. In Mexicali, life was a lot harder for Amá. She had to wake even earlier to get a seat on the work truck. There was not enough room for all of the workers, so every morning was a competition just to get a seat. Once her workday was over, she had to rush home to prepare Apá's police uniform, as he had left the fields for the police force in Mexicali two years after he moved there.

His uniform had to look immaculate every day, as if it had never been worn before. There was not one wrinkle, and every crease was starched to perfection. He demanded that his brass police badge must glisten in the sun like a piece of glass. Having to cater to Apá's obsession with his appearance was hard for all of us to comprehend. Every day when it was time for him to leave for work, we would watch Amá bend down and wipe his already shiny shoes. Upon leaving the house, he always walked right in the middle of the road.

On our street there was a green house hidden behind a mass of trees. This house held a secret. A dark man with an enormous stomach lived in this house. He had shifty eyes that he never fully exposed, shading them behind sunglasses as he disguised himself under a big white sombrero. The dark evil of his being was transparent to us even through this camouflage. Amá warned us never to go near him, but she had no idea of how evil he really was. When we walked home from school, preparing to pass by his house, Mary made sure we held each other's hands. Unconsciously we tried to outrun the dirty feeling we picked up from his surroundings, but no pace was fast enough.

As we came near his house we developed the instincts of wary animals. We knew he was dangerous, we felt the filth of his unnamed cravings and the starvation in his eyes. He knew when his prey would pass by. He knew that a mother's energy was spent on days of backbreaking labor, and that knowledge of the whereabouts of her children was a luxury often beyond her. If a child was sick, or hurt, or lost for a day, this might be the least of a mother's troubles. Her concern was focused on the roof over their head, the food on the table, the hours of work needed to cover the bills.

This beast invited children into his house. We saw them come out later with money. Around grown-ups he was a man of a different face. He would walk straight, with his head up, as if he had nothing to hide.

Estella was the one to unveil his secret. One day Estella was tempted by his offer of five dollars. She was with a friend who knew what to expect, but Estella didn't. When the fat, sweating man asked them to come into his house and take their panties off, my sister ran out of his house and straight home. She looked so frightened, as if she had seen a ghost. We didn't tell Amá about sick men like him in the neighborhood, for fear of being punished for provoking them. Maybe if we had told, we could have prevented children from being molested by them.

In this house, too, is where I gave Lisa her first big haircut. Lisa stayed with Abuelita Demetria when we lived in Mexicali. Each time we picked up Lisa to stay with us for the weekend, her waist-length hair would be matted and dirty. After Mary gave her a bath, her long, beautifully curly locks would bounce as she walked. I had curly, nappy hair that grew only to the sides—I was never given the choice of cutting it or not. Mary decided when it was time and would bring out her tin bowl. She would place the bowl over my head and cut around it. I was dark and skinny, and with that haircut I looked like a boy.

Lisa had thick eyelashes, and her eyes were dark and penetrating, like little marbles. When I was left in charge of Lisa,

I'd take her outside to play. I guess I grew envious because every time we were outside, one passerby after another would say about her, "Oh, what a beautiful little girl." This time, instead of going outside, I had a better idea. I pulled a wooden box up to the kitchen table. Many times before I had sat her at this table to color, but this time it was different. I sat her there while I gave her a "new look."

I took out the big, old, rusted pair of heavy shears and began hacking away at her hair. I started with her bangs, clipping at the hairline, and then followed the growth of her hair, close to the scalp. It took me quite a while, but Lisa sat there obediently, even though her eyes kept getting bigger as she watched the pile of hair on the floor grow. I tried distracting her with a banana, but she stared harder at the hair falling to the floor. Suddenly I realized that what I was doing was wrong. At the same time, I heard the door open and there stood Joe. He was horrified at the scene before him. So, now, was I. When my eyes met his, I knew without a word that I was in big trouble.

How well I recall, too, the warm and happy memories of those old days, and the building of our house in Mexicali. When I close my eyes I can still hear our laughter and picture four little girls plastered with mud from head to toe, our eyelashes heavy with caked mud. The building began on one of those blistering hot days when we had gone to the American canal to swim. While we were gone, Apá started to prepare the adobe mix. After we returned, he told us we could come help him stomp the soil and mix it with the straw. He did not have to tell us twice—we all jumped in. Many of our days were taken up with the mud-stomping work. When the mix was ready, we moved to the next step, molding blocks from our mix. It was not long before we had hundreds of blocks.

Regardless of what we were doing, Apá would make big plans with us. Our days passed quickly as we all shared our lists of wants. It was a make-believe world. Whatever we asked for,

Apá was going to do, or he was going to get what we wanted. We all had big illusions and wishes. Maybe Estella would get a bike, or I would get china dishes for my doll, or Mary would have her own bed. One thing I loved about Apá was that he always said "yes" to everything we asked for, even though he never followed through. We always had our fantasies.

Queena

Once, before fiesta time, when Apá was listening to all of our hopes, he told us he had a big surprise and would reveal it on the coming Friday. Crazy and anxious from such big news, we told him we could not wait. I thought the anticipation of Friday night would kill us all.

Almost an hour later than expected that Friday, we heard the sound of an engine, our father's engine. We ran out to the street to greet him as he scrambled out of his truck. He was wearing the most beautiful, mischievous smile, his gold teeth shining and his eyes filled with glee. It did not take us more than a second to notice that he was carrying a big burlap sack.

"What's in it? What is it?" we all yelled. He told us we would have to guess. We knew it had to be some sort of animal because we could see something wiggling around in the bag. We guessed that it was either a puppy or a rabbit. We knew it wasn't a kitten because my mother did not like cats. My father knew he was torturing us with this game, so he gave in and opened the sack. The cutest little black-and-white piglet we could imagine was curled up inside, shivering with fear. Apá said it would be our pet as long as we were responsible for it. We named this new treasure Queena.

Queena's first days with us were difficult for her. She found it hard to adjust to her new surroundings. The absence of her mother made her whine, but soon her cries became whimpers of happiness from all of our attention and feeding. My *apá* and *tío* made a pen for her, and she quickly became the neighborhood pet. In the meantime, we watched the house grow brick by brick, and as the house got bigger, Queena got bigger and fatter.

When the construction of the house was complete, we knew there would be more things to do before this home would become ours. A fiesta was in the making. In the morning, my father sent us to my aunt's house. When we returned home, the smell of roasting meat had driven the dogs in the vicinity into a manic barking, all at the same time. Brightly colored paper decorations excited the eye. The street was blocked with tables, perfectly lined up, dressed with white cloths and vases full of paper flowers, hot pink and red carnations big as chrysanthemums. Streamers of every color hung around the dancing area. It looked as if the governor might be stopping by. Some of Apá's friends arrived early and sat around these tables overindulging in mountainous plates of rice, beans, and red *moles* with steamy corn tortillas. Those who were not chewing picked their teeth or licked the grease from their mustaches, while others with bellies about to explode belched and declared how delicious the food was.

The ladies, including my *amá*, who had looked like housemaids when we left, were now transformed into further attractions of the fiesta. Some were dressed in happy colors—red and black taffeta—and others in beautiful white brocaded materials. Some looked truly festive. Others overdid it, with fake diamonds cascading into their cleavage as their breasts hung like ripe pears, squeezed into too tight dresses stretched across their protruding stomachs. There were ladies with wide, round bottoms that seemed to go on forever, rippling like a tide. Their slinky spike-heeled shoes looked as if they were choking the feet that wore them.

While not all of their appearances were perfect to the eye or beautiful from the outside, this was soon overshadowed by the richness of the ladies' laughter. Their zest for fiesta spread like wildfire among the others who might be asleep on the inside, and soon they all floated together with the music. With the excitement of the fiesta, they even forgot about their children, who eventually fell asleep under chairs and tables, their faces licked like candy by the dogs.

The strumming of guitars was announcement enough that the fiesta had begun. Everyone stomped their feet and clouds of dust arose from the dance floor. Waves of happiness, craziness, drenched them as music and laughter coursed through their bodies until there was no one left sitting down. Once everyone was dancing, the real music began. Trumpets blared, and the clarinets' shrill voice filled the air while wild Mexican lyrics lifted up the hearts of all. Voices grew louder and louder as more bottles dropped to the floor. Everyone became the lead singer. The anger and passion of daily life were transformed into a frenzy of happiness during fiesta, and the happiness did not end until the mariachis played the last song. Some did not even make it home that night, sleeping contentedly on chairs and tables.

The next morning Joe awoke bright and early, as always. Something seemed oddly different to him. He walked around the new house, but found everything in place. Then he realized it was the noise, or rather the lack of noise, that disturbed him. He did not hear Queena's morning oinking. He ran to her pen, only to find the usual flies buzzing around. In shock, he ran through the house and pushed open his parents' bedroom door. Knowing that he could fix anything, he frantically shook his father's arm to wake him, to beg him to find Queena for us. Soon his sisters were at his side. Amá, from her side of the bed, shot Apá a look of purest recrimination. She took a deep breath, filling her lungs with rage. We could see her muscles tighten as she desperately clenched her jaw shut. She waited for him to explain this mystery to us, but there was only silence. Finally he could see there was no way out of this, even for him, and he lowered his eyes and said, "Children, we ate her last night."

After so much hard work and sacrifice, our home was built. Amá gave it the last touches, planting a start of ivy, which one day, she thought, would grow and cover the exterior wall. Next to where Apá had built the cement planters, she had also planted four small trees, often saying, "I'll nurture them now so that I will have them in my old age."

Amá never got to enjoy her ivy or her trees in old age. Neither did Apá ever get to enjoy the house he had worked to build. The price he paid for his ways was to become homeless, endlessly roaming from place to place like a tortured soul. Amá was so right when she said, "*Lo que se empieza mal, acaba mal.*" ("That which begins badly, ends badly.")

Joe and the Pool Hall
~

Not long after the completion of the house in Mexicali, Joe was on his way home one evening when he stopped at Barrio's Pool Hall. It was in a big, old, windowless plywood building, its only light provided by single-bulb lamps dangling from ceiling cords. The light just emphasized the smoke in the atmosphere. Young boys wandered between the pool tables selling home-roasted sunflower seeds. Others sat in corners waiting to shine shoes. The players, all men, stood about drinking from bottles of beer, swearing, laughing. Joe was standing at a pool table enjoying the men's conversation and the excitement of the game when Apá happened to pass by the door. As it happened, he glanced inside and spotted his son.

Instead of stopping and bringing Joe home, he continued on his way, growing angrier with every step. By the time he arrived home, he was beside himself. He told my mother he was not going to have a *pachuco* ("a worthless son") or a *pildora* ("a pill-popper") living under his roof. When Joe arrived home soon after Apá, my father reprimanded him. If he ever caught Joe inside that place again, Joe would pay the consequences. Joe stood there, stone-faced and silent. Barrio's was the main hangout for the guys at that time, and Joe felt trapped between wanting to be with his friends and not daring to defy his father. For all his sins, my father still criticized the men who went to Barrio's, calling them lowlifes who would never amount to anything, who only stood on the corner to look good.

A couple of weeks later, the same thing happened again. My sisters and I were standing next to an adobe house, scraping off the mud and chewing on it. We were driven to do it by malnutrition and the lack of certain minerals in our diet, although we did not know the reason at the time. We saw my *apá* get off the city bus on the corner, and we ran excitedly to greet him just as we did every day, full of the innocent and constantly renewed love that children have for their parents at that age. But Apá was too furious to acknowledge us. We knew something was wrong. At home he paced back and forth, mumbling to himself. By the time Joe got home, Apá had had enough time to charge up his fury and was waiting for him on the patio. Apá exploded, screaming at Joe that he was worthless, like the men in the pool hall. He didn't even give him a chance to gather his belongings before he threw him out of the house. Joe stood in front of Apá for a moment, looked him straight in the eye, and left without a word.

We didn't understand what was going on and followed Joe into the street, crying. Finally he told us to go back home, promising that he would come back for us soon. When we refused, he ordered Mary to take us home. And so she did. In the tense hours that followed there was an eerie quiet surrounding the whole house. Amá stood clutching her apron in one hand, stirring a pot with another, tears rolling down her cheeks. When she saw us, she wiped her eyes. She would not let us ask or talk about what had happened. She would only shush us, "Quiet, here comes your father."

I have often asked myself what was Joe's real motive in going back to the pool hall. Was it just the social need of a teenager? Or did he take the opportunity to be free of his parents' household? He might well have claimed the right to be a man, since he had never had the right to be a child. He moved to the room Amá had rented in Calexico, right across the border, to keep a U.S. address. He found a job at Jimmy's Grocery Store and shifted the night job he already had to days, so that now he could work two jobs. He was able to make a life for himself, but the price was an aging of his heart and soul. He was thirteen years old.

It was an extremely hot day, that one day in Mexicali when Apá came home with a present for Mary. It was not unusual for him to single out his favorite girl. She was like his most beautiful shining star in a dark, peaceful night. He thought of us other three girls too, but he would only bring us a piece of fruit, and if we were asleep he would wrap it inside our arms. We would wake up to an apple or banana. But Mary would always wake up to something special.

This time the present was a little red-and-white clay cow

that cost about eighty cents. I was perhaps four-and-a-half. When I saw it I immediately wanted it. Mary grabbed it away and told me not to touch it because it was hers. I was angry and shouted back that I was going to break it when she was gone. My father heard me say this, and he warned me that if anything happened to the little clay cow, he would give me a spanking.

While all this was going on, Estella and some of the neighborhood kids were getting ready to go to the waterfalls, where we often spent afternoons trying to stay cool like many other families. This time it was not my turn to go. I watched the old truck disappear down the dusty road, and forgot about the red-and-white cow. The cow stayed where Mary had left it, on top of the ironing board. I took off running to a neighbor's house, found some children my age, and down the street we went barefoot. By the time we finished playing it was impossible to guess the original color of my shorts and blouse, they were so covered in mud. My scalp felt like sandpaper with all the dirt in my hair, but we were intensely happy, forgetting about time.

That was also the day that Alice had been there, the ironing lady who came twice a month to press my *apá*'s uniforms. She accidentally broke the red clay cow, but her job was finished before Apá and the girls got back, and she left without telling anyone about it.

When they got back from the falls, I was still in the street playing. I saw Estella rush toward me, trembling, already anticipating the beating I was to get from Apá. She called me to come quickly because I was in trouble. How right she was. When I got home, there was Apá standing outside on the porch, holding in his hand a rope that was used to tie up horses.

As I came closer to him, I saw him take the rope and entwine it around his fingers. With his other hand he pointed at a spot in front of him. He was telling me, "Stand here."

Although he still hadn't touched me, I knew I was going to be hurt. It was not hard to tell when Apá was angry, because his hair stood on end and his dark skin would get darker, almost purple.

I heard him ask me why I broke the cow after he had warned me not to touch it. I heard him say, *"Muchacha, te voy a quitar lo necio."* ("Girl, I'm going to take care of your stubbornness.") I tried to tell him I didn't do it, but he didn't hear me. The last thing I remember doing was closing my eyes and clenching my body as I saw the rope swing down toward me. I must have made myself travel to a place of no pain, because when I opened my eyes and looked up, I saw Amá kneeling on the floor next to me, bending to soothe the raw ridges left on my body. Apá was no longer there when my brother Joe arrived.

As he did many afternoons, Joe had come around to check on us. What he found that day so incensed him that he resolved on the spot to move us away from Apá. He yelled at my mother, "How can you live with a man who treats us like this?" He ordered Mary and Estella to put their shoes on, to put some stuff together, because we were getting out of there. They were both racing against the clock, gathering together their few belongings before Apá could return home acting like nothing had happened, and we would no longer be able to leave.

Amá followed her children around the house pleading with them to wait. Joe said we had already waited too long and he was going to take us all away once and for all. She could stay if she wanted to, but the children were not going to have to take that kind of treatment from Apá anymore.

Everything happened so fast. We all put on our plastic sandals, and finally Amá threw some of her working clothes in a paper sack. We hurried to the bus stop four houses away from our brown house. We were lucky—the bus pulled up at the same time we did.

It had taken ten months to build the house of Amá's dreams and three months for her same dream to be shattered forever. I never again heard her speak about owning a house. We were out on the road again. In about twenty minutes we had crossed the border into Calexico. We cried all the way. We were both terrified of Apá and terrified to leave him behind. My brother kept reassuring us that we would be okay, that he would take care of us.

Soon we arrived at our place of refuge. Joe brought us back to the little room that Amá had rented to give us a school address. This single room didn't look any different from the sun-bleached, dried-out shack you'd pass in the desert and wonder who in the world lived there. It was a strange feeling when my brother opened the door and said, "This is our new home."

We immediately started to ask, as we looked around, "Where is the kitchen?" and "Where are we going to sleep?" He pointed out the kitchen, which consisted of a kerosene stove that he had placed on a wooden crate in the corner of the room. Next to it was a round wooden table with two more milk crates that were used for chairs. The sleeping quarters were on the other side of the wall, where we found an old steel army cot with one green wool blanket and a flat feather pillow. Joe could tell by the expressions on our faces that we were wondering where we could all sleep. He pointed to the floor, "Right here. Some will sleep on the floor and some on the bed."

From inside the house you could see the broken, narrow, crumbling sidewalk and the waves of heat from the dry, thirsty ground. The street was a constant reminder of what we thought we had left behind—a poor neighborhood.

I was lucky and got to sleep in the bed with Joe. I suffered from rheumatism, and many nights I would wake up crying in pain. My *amá* would soak a towel in kerosene and wrap my knee and put me in bed with Joe, where I would keep warm with his legs on top of my knees.

The time we lived in that house is one of faded memories

of both parents. It felt like we had none. We had left Apá behind, and Amá was always gone, leaving the house earlier every day to follow the crops where they took her, returning home when we were asleep. Sometimes she worked through the next day. Her absence caused me to stay home alone in the morning, and I was too young to understand the reasons. Joe had enrolled Mary and Estella in school all day, while I attended kindergarten in the afternoon.

The first day I cried. I hated for the morning to come when I'd be left alone. For a while I felt as if I was being punished, locked in a cage with one tiny ray of light coming in through a small window and fearful sounds coming through the warped walls. How quickly a child forgets the beatings and the terror of the past. Instead of being happy to escape the abuse at Apá's hands, inside this tiny cage I longed for the freedom that existed outside my window.

And still my mother was crossing the border to see Apá. She would go over and stay the weekends, asking the lady next door to please keep an eye on us. We cried because we didn't want her to leave us. We wanted to follow, but Joe would say no, he didn't want us to fall into the same trap again. He tried to make us all feel better by giving us each a quarter. And if we were really good and didn't fight with each other, he'd bring home a package of sweet rolls.

Joe was fifteen. Because of his pride and dignity he prevented Amá from getting welfare. He provided a safe little home away from the threats of beatings. She had a little bed of her own. We had food on the table. In Joe's view, Amá had everything she needed. But still she persisted in visiting Apá across the border. Looking back, as adults, Joe and I have many times discussed, "What kind of *perro* ('doglike') love did Amá have for him?" I wonder, was she like a bird locked in a cage that wouldn't leave even when the door was opened? How strange it is when we are frozen to the familiar, even when it brings us harm.

The Cellar

~

I am bewildered. I have lost the memory of why we moved out of the faded brown room in Calexico. Why can I not remember? I must know! I ask my sisters but they don't know. I call Joe at home and ask, "Joe, tell me why we left the one-room house."

He answers with a question, his voice trembling. "Why do you need to know?"

"I'm trying to make some sense out of my memories. Joe, did we ever live in a cellar?" Actually, my sad recollection is more of a dungeon. All of a sudden the line goes quiet.

"Joe, are you okay? Are you still on the line? I know you tried to take care of all of us, but what happened?"

"We were evicted because we didn't have the twelve damned dollars a month to pay them. Our neighbor, Lola, let us stay in the cellar under her house. It was entered from the outside. We had to walk down a few steps to that big, dark, putrid-smelling dirt floor room. We had no window. What we had for light was a couple of small candles.

"We followed Mary for protection everywhere she walked because there were spiders and spider webs wherever we turned. The entrance to the cellar was a remnant of the old, crumbling foundation. The rotten runoff water leaked through cracks in the walls and ceiling.

"The view we had inside was still better than the one we had when we walked outdoors. Outside of this hovel we met with a barrage of garbage, overfilled trash cans, piles of refuse in the alley. The smells were worse than a dump."

"How long did we live there?"

"Just until Amá and I were able to save enough money to move into Billy's Apartments."

As my brother spoke, vivid memories came to the surface. I began to relive the cellar, to feel what it was like to be there. I had felt myself to be a child nobody wanted, a disposable child thrown into the garbage. I remember wanting to tell the world that my family and I had a right to live and deserved a home. We were good and worked hard.

"Are you still there?" Joe asks.

"Yes. Wait. These old memories are new to me." I taste tears in my mouth, feel a battle within my heart. "So this is why I get that mourning feeling when I pass a place similar to that one."

These are the images that come to mind when I think of the years that followed in Billy's white apartments. In my mind I feel like we are caught in a deep river. Crowds of people are standing by, watching my three sisters and me struggle to keep from drowning. We see people observing us with dead eyes. No one moves. We fight the swirling waters, bobbing up for breath, only to have a gigantic wave hit us from behind . . . still no response from those watching. We surrender to the pull and suddenly the water disappears. Now we are standing on dry desert ground, safe from one danger. Our bodies seem whole, but something inside us has changed forever.

Many things happened in the eight years we lived there. Sometimes we children were forced to survive by scavenging or somehow earning our own food. As we struggled just to meet our basic needs, our neighbors took it upon themselves to tell Amá when we failed to meet their standards, knowing that any complaint would bring us severe punishment. *"Mira, Elisa. Tu muchacha grosera no me saludó."* ("Look, Elisa. Your stupid daughter didn't give me a greeting.") Neglecting to treat a neighbor with "due" respect would bring a beating with a belt. Sadly, we feared our own family members more than anyone because they were the ones who abused us the most. We grew up angry and wary like barn cats, developing a tough skin in self-defense.

Having once conquered the relatives, the next battle for us was the neighbors. Generally children are sent to school to learn, but in our attempts to learn we were constantly ridiculed. Whether it was what we wore, what we said, or what we didn't say, we were constantly reminded of how stupid they thought we were, how we failed to conform to their expectations. And this from our own kind!

Billy's six apartments looked flimsy and run-down. None of them was larger than one bedroom with three windows and a small kitchen. Our apartment had three beds, each showing the shapes of our bodies. Estella and Amá slept in one, Mary and I in another, and since Lisa lived with Abuelita, Joe had his own.

This is what life was like in this apartment: the noises, voices, and smells all mingled together like an open market, with everyone knowing everyone else's business. Life began at four A.M. when, in the apartment next to us, the same tune was sung every morning, the same door was slammed. A frantic mother tripped over her own feet, her high-pitched voice shouting, "Wake up your brother and don't be late for school!" She herself would often forget her lunch as she rushed to the truck, barely making it before the rail door slammed shut.

On the other side of us came a different tune from a different mother. Busy with her hands rolling tacos while her mind was on the children, she would shout, "Don't forget to change your underwear today!" Meanwhile her tacos would burn. At the same time, another woman could be heard calling out to whoever might hear her, "Hey, does anyone have a can of tomatoes I can borrow?" These wild mornings seemed so normal to us.

This is also where we lived when I started first grade. The summer had seemed long to me. I thought that tomorrow would never come. I was finally going to be in the same school with my sisters. The first day of school, Amá made sure we all looked fresh and new, like the rest of the children. I felt proud and beautiful to be dressed like Mary in a pretty, white floral cotton dress with an umbrella skirt and stiff petticoat. Mary would complain to Amá that she was too old to be dressed the same as her little sister. Amá answered that it was better this way. I know what she meant: The only way we could all have new dresses was for Amá to purchase a quantity of the same material for her dollar. Our identical outfits labeled us as being from the same family. That prompted Stella to nick-name me Alice because the name Ercenia embarrassed her.

My first day at school didn't turn out to be as joyous as I had anticipated. I ended up being terrified of the teacher. I was so afraid of her and her screaming that to this day I do not remember what she looked like, or if I ever learned any-thing of what she tried to teach us. She spent the entire day threatening one student or another. I began to dread going to school. I accepted being frightened until she tried to teach us how to tell time. I was not a fast learner. She was impatient with me when she'd ask me the time and I'd give her the wrong answer. She would yell at me and ask me if I was stupid. I would become scared and start to cry. This was the first time I had felt the emotion of embarrassment. I didn't know the name for the feeling, but I learned it later in life.

I would go home and ask Joe to teach me to tell time. Lacking the skills, he would try to explain to me, and then holler and hit me when I gave a wrong answer. He would punch me in the head with his fist, using his middle knuckle for emphasis.

But not everything was grim. Life has a way of evening things out. It was here in Billy's Apartments that we experi-enced our own Christmas miracle. The other houses in the neighborhood had started putting up their Christmas decora-tions. We could see their lighted Christmas trees from out-side. There was no sign that Amá was going to buy a tree, but Mary decided we would have our tree too. She made us find a coffee can and fill it with dirt. Estella cut a tree branch and stuck it in the coffee can. We hung cotton ball chains and necklaces around the tree for decoration.

We were very proud of our tree, so we stuck it in our front window like the neighbors did. We didn't care that our tree was bare of presents, unlike the others. On Christmas Eve, we could hear the church bells ringing and sense the happiness that came with the holiday. As we sat around our little home-made tree, we saw a six-foot-tall, decorated Christmas tree walking up to our front door. When the door opened, there was Joe, carrying it inside. Mrs. Brown, the director of the neighborhood club, had grown fond of us and was giving us the tree. At a quarter to midnight, there came a knock at the door. My mother opened it and there stood Santa Claus! He carried a big basket of food and a present for each of us. We each received a powder puff with a tiny bottle of perfume on top. Later I learned that good old Santa belonged to the Salvation Army.

In this place, Billy's Apartments, we also learned about hunger. When it wasn't crop time, Amá could hardly make enough money for the rent. The apartments were behind Jimmy's Grocery Store, and late on Monday nights, when Amá thought no one was around, she would send Estella and me to the dumpster in search of food. Sometimes we would find chunks of pig fat or moldy pieces of bacon strips. Amá would cut the chunks and make them into pork rinds. She would save the lard to cook with the rest of the week. Sometimes we would find beef intestines. Amá would cook them all day and mix them with hot salsa. That was how we survived those lean times.

She thought that Jimmy wasn't aware of us digging in his garbage, but now I think he must have known, because later there were whole boxes of tomatoes and chiles that weren't good enough to be sold. Out of the big boxes of chiles he gave us, only a dozen or so vegetables would be edible. And when weevils got into the flour, Jimmy would save it for my mother because he knew she could work with it.

Regardless of how long and hard Amá worked, it just wasn't enough to survive. As we got older, we would help by ironing a dozen pillowcases for a dollar. When the ironing was done, we'd fold clothes or anything else to help the day move along faster. We never got paid on the same day, so my mother would keep a little log of all the hours worked and the clothes that were ironed. This was pointless because she never received the money that she had truly earned. On many occasions, we weren't even paid with money. Sometimes people would pass off their junk on us, thinking we would jump for joy when we received old shoes or rotten food.

One time Amá came home with what I thought was a big, fat, moldy tortilla smothered in tomato sauce with hard cheese stuck to it. It turned out to be a pizza. My mother would return with these "goodies" very depressed. Friends would always say to her, "Elisa, why don't you just say something?" She never did, though, just hoping she would be paid in money the next week.

In third grade I met my best friend, Silvia. This girl had a soft white complexion. Her hair was long and black and often up in ponytails wrapped with ribbons that matched her outfit. When she got excited her cheeks turned pink and she smiled with her whole face. I looked totally the opposite of her, but our spirits were the same. Many hours of our childhood were spent together.

Silvia lived four blocks from our apartment. She had everything I didn't have—a house, a white picket fence, a yard with grass and flowers. When we entered her house, her cocker spaniel would greet us. The living room was completely furnished, and each member of the family had his or her own bedroom. Silvia's room was like a page out of a fairy-tale book. It had every color that makes the heart happy. Wooden plaques of Snow White and the Seven Dwarfs marched across the wall. There seemed to be half of the stuffed animal kingdom here, fuzzy and colorful. No one could have felt alone in that room, she had so many baby dolls with open arms begging to be picked up and loved. The ones I felt a need to hold were the ones with blue eyes, like the people I had noticed on the street with light eyes. I thought they were blind and I pitied them.

Silvia had one of the few mothers who stayed home and didn't go out to work. Her mother would look after her after school with a snack in the refrigerator. Silvia was the only one of my friends who could talk to her mother as an equal and not get her face slapped. She spoke to her in the familiar *tú*, like friends of the same age, and was actually brave enough to question her mother's orders.

I liked Lupe, Silvia's mother, although she was hard to comprehend and her peculiar way of thinking confused me. She was known as snooty and mean because all she did was complain. That was as far as it went. Whenever I went home with Silvia after school, it wasn't long before we were in trouble with her mother. Silvia hadn't changed out of her school clothes, or we had gone into the parents' bedroom. Lupe's face would grow purple and her throat veins pop out as she followed us through the house, wagging her finger, hollering, "Just you wait, wait till your father gets home. I am going to tell him how rude you were to me!" Silvia played deaf. "Don't worry," she would tell me, "by the time my father gets home she'll have forgotten."

I never learned what kinds of people were acceptable to Lupe. She made Silvia cry on many occasions when she wouldn't let her go out and play with us. Silvia would argue and want to know why. Lupe would answer, "*¿No tienes miedo que se te pegue lo negro?*" ("Aren't you afraid their black will rub off on you?") Tears in her eyes, Silvia would answer truthfully, "*Sí, pero yo las quiero mucho.*" ("Yes, but I love them so much.")

And then Silvia would observe, *"Pero, si tú también estás prieta, ¿qué te crees muy blanca?"* ("But you're dark too, or do you think you're white?")

Lupe was in denial about her coloring. Her skin was the color of milk chocolate, mine semisweet. But Lupe was obsessed with being white. She used layers of pancake makeup to cover her age spots and worked hard to keep up with her black roots, using an ash blond preparation that turned a brassy blond on her.

Silvia's grandfather rode by every midmorning on his bicycle with a big smile on his face and a basket of fresh hot tamales strapped to the back. Grandpa dressed in faded work clothes like every other man in the neighborhood, but he was different. He had a gift of humor, and he used it to bring smiles to the dried-up faces of the old women who sat like motionless scarecrows under the trees, gazing into the distance. He also delighted the dogs. At the smell of the tamales and the sound of his whistling, they perked up their noses and began to dance, lifting their heads to receive his pats.

Whenever we came upon him, he was singing or talking to himself. Silvia would wave him down, shouting, "Abuelito! Abuelito!" She wouldn't stop till he came to the door and gave her money, slipping his hand into his pocket for change and always making the same remark, *"Muchacha*, you're eating up my profit."

What I envied most, however, was Silvia's relationship with her father. He gave her everything and was never afraid to show his love for her. Whatever she did, he didn't make a big fuss or frighten her so bad that she begged God to turn her body into stone so that beatings couldn't be felt. She was his "sunshine," his "magic star," and "the most beautiful princess in the world." He used these phrases whenever she walked into the room. She shared this love with me and often gave me clothes she didn't use anymore. My favorite was a big, round Easter hat. It was white with navy blue trim and two wide satin ribbons that hung down my back. The prettiest thing about it was the big, white crushed rose in back. I wore this hat every day, with everything, until Amá finally had to throw it away.

I got a spanking many times because I didn't want to return home. We had seen the many toys and pretty clothes of our classmates. We did not hide from Amá how badly we wanted nice things. I thought she didn't understand, since we didn't receive them, but she wasn't blind. She could see that we didn't have the things that our friends had. Looking back, I realize now how hard she tried to compensate for those things. The paychecks she didn't receive were a constant reminder of the things she could have given us. She would tell us that if we worked very hard she would give us a little gift at the end of the week. She often had to break those promises, and we never really knew how hard this was for her. These were the times I wished I had a father, a real father who could help us. I wanted to know why we had to be so poor.

Dental care was something we could not afford. One irritatingly humid, hot day Estella complained of a toothache. At midnight her endless sobbing awakened me. I got up from the floor half-asleep and followed the cry. As I got closer, I heard Mary begging Estella to stop crying. She was afraid Joe would come home from work and hit her because she couldn't stop Estella's pain. Mary had already tried all the remedies Amá had taught her for toothache pain, but nothing seemed to work. Mary had rubbed *yerba buena* on the inside of the tooth and put hot cloths on Estella's little face. The infection had caused one side of her face to swell, and now she couldn't stop crying. Mary became desperate and hit her.

Joe saw Estella being mistreated and immediately regained control of the situation the best way he knew how—by smacking Mary. But Joe had made Mary responsible for everything that happened to her little sisters. If other kids hit us at school, Joe used a thin leather belt on Mary for letting such things happen. When chores weren't finished, Joe became angry with Mary for not seeing to it that they were completed. Whether she had done her own chores didn't count. Since Joe was out of the house all day, he needed to know that someone was overseeing us.

Estella's luck was not very good that year. In third grade she got the short teacher with the hard, severe look about her that matched the sharp lines of her face, her stern, authoritative voice. Her demeanor was cruel to the core. In 1954, when we were in school, it was not acceptable for girls to wear pants to class. During that time we were lucky if we had two outfits to wear. We would wash out our clothes at night and wear them again the next day. We were also required to wear a slip, but since we could not afford them, Estella would wear one of Joe's white T-shirts. When Estella's name was called at roll call, the teacher would ask her, "Why do you always have to look like a tramp?" Estella would cry in silence, because she knew nobody would listen to her if she admitted how much this hurt.

As if one year with this woman wasn't enough, Estella failed third grade and had to spend another year with the same teacher. When Estella learned she had failed, she was afraid to come home with her report card because she knew it meant we would all be whipped. Evening came and there was still no sign of Estella. Suddenly we saw a movement under the bed. There she was. As she crawled slowly out from underneath, she looked like a scared cat facing a dog many times its size. She lifted herself from the floor and meekly handed her report card to Joe. He was already armed with the leather belt, prepared to make it dance on Estella's back. As he attacked her with the belt, Estella just stood stoically, turning her body from side to side, letting him whip her. It was always the one who wasn't being hit who cried the hardest, making it sound as if Joe were killing all of us.

Vultures

~

One extremely hot afternoon I saw my *amá* walking very slowly. She always looked tired, but this time her face looked sickly and she seemed to walk with great pain. Her mouth was dry. We could see the whiteness around her lips; her skin tinged a sweaty yellow. As her friend walked her to the house, she told us that they had had to stop the truck. Amá had passed out. We thought it was caused either by exertion and dehydration from working in the fields, or that it had been caused by the overcrowded conditions of the picker trucks.

The back of these trucks was made of wooden planks and had no ventilation. They were intended for the transport of animals, not people—but men, women, and children rode these trucks daily between work and home. It was always a nauseating ride, sliding back and forth, battering each other, and breathing in everyone else's body odors, the smell of their lunches and the stale smell of trucks that were never washed. Every time we hit a winding road, our bodies would bang from one side to another, causing us to land on each other. Sometimes we would come home with bruises on our backs because of the screw heads sticking out of the wooden slats of the truck. Often we were already sore before we started the day's work.

We thought this was the trouble now with Amá. I felt bad for her; she looked so fragile and about ready to collapse. As often as we asked her, "Are you okay?" her answer was always, "Yes, I'm okay."

She showered and put on her thin housecoat. She didn't ask if we had done our chores or how our day went. She threw herself on the bare linoleum in front of the fan. She asked us to bring a wet cloth to place on her head and stomach. We asked her if she wanted to eat. "No. Just let me rest for a bit."

We were really worried when she didn't go to her second job. Night fell and it was time for all of us to go to bed. We could see Amá tossing and turning from side to side, moaning, "Ay, ay, ay." Several times in the night, we heard her get up and walk from the door to the little sink, pacing. In the morning, she had us call one of the neighbors to come over and take her to a doctor. As it turned out, she needed emergency gall bladder surgery.

Before he would operate, the doctor wanted to know who would be paying for his services. When he realized we had no money, his office contacted the welfare office. Then the surgery was done. After Amá was home for several days a white car arrived, a car with some sort of picture on the side of the door. We later learned that it was a government symbol. A large, fat lady got out of the car carrying papers. Striding up to our door, she stood at the entrance of our house and surveyed it with beady eyes. We felt threatened by her. Her attitude was as big as her body.

Accompanying this social worker was a translator. With no exchange of words, she rummaged in her folder, took out a notepad, and began writing rapidly, as if she were taking inventory of the whole house. After talking to my Amá, she announced that she thought it would be best if we were all placed in foster homes. She did not approve of the conditions in which we lived. We knew it wasn't much, but our house was clean. As the sweaty lady walked out, she tried to pry further information from us. She wanted to know if there were any other men coming or going from our house besides our brother. The fat lady might as well have accused my *amá* of adultery. Amá began to cry. This was a terrible insult to her. We did not understand exactly what was going on, but we felt Amá's fear. Amá was terrified of this woman and so were we.

When the fat woman left, Amá sent us to hide at the neighbors' house. From their window, we could peek out to see if the fat woman had come back. When we were sure she had gone, we noticed other neighbor women standing outside their doors. They stared at us like vultures, starving for gossip, wanting to fulfill some insatiable need. They asked us, "What is happening to you kids?" Their questions made us certain we had done something wrong. We felt suddenly unsafe, afraid of being torn apart. Yet we could not understand what we had done wrong.

The round circle on the car door was a government symbol. Amá told us not to open the door to that woman again. It was a long time before we felt safe.

The welfare people must have spoken to the school, because suddenly we received lunch tickets. We were really happy that we no longer had to walk home for lunch, being able to share lunch break with the rest of the students. Our happiness didn't last long, however. The free lunch tickets were a different color from the purchased ones. When the other children saw our charity tickets, they made fun of us. We threw the rest of the wrong-colored tickets away and never told our mother. That was the end of the lunch tickets.

It was a shame and a real loss to us all that we Mexicans, being of the same race, didn't try to help one another. We could have encouraged each other, for to set another free is to set yourself free. It makes me think back to when all of the pickers were in the truck and the foreman lifted the rail up and shouted, "*¿Órale ya? Están todos los animales adentro?*" ("Are all the animals inside?") This foreman was like the thief who sees a half-blind, crippled old lady walking down the street with nothing but her cane to hold on to and, for no reason, grabs the cane and runs off with it. He enjoyed kicking us while we were down.

It was at this time that the American government offered Apá his second chance to return to the United States and obtain his immigration papers. This was under one condition:

that he would take full responsibility for his family and that he would remain in the country for a period of time without crossing the border. He was offered this opportunity because of Amá's illness, because we needed him more than ever for economic support.

It is still unbelievable to me that he refused the opportunity. How could he be so heartless? He had taken us to the hell of Calexico from Salinas, from a land that had provided us with everything we needed, only to abandon us once more. Now it was an easy choice for him. He simply replied, "Nobody can keep me away from my *tierra*." When he made that clear choice, right then and there, the officers promptly revoked his visa. His selfish desire for his homeland brought his children to shame and poverty in Imperial Valley.

Apá
~

The day Apá rejected his wife and children for his country, he became dead to Mary. Amá was too sick to take care of us, and Apá had been given the chance to come back and provide for us, but he refused. From that day on, his name was never on her lips. Whenever any adult or friend would ask her, "Mary, where is your *papá*? We haven't seen him," she would look that person straight in the face and answer, "My *papá* died in the war." And quickly change the subject.

Estella and I still kept our *apá* alive, but it wasn't for very long. We went to Mexicali and looked for him where he said he would be, but he never showed up. For a while, we didn't mind playing hide-and-go-seek with him because it was the only hope we had of getting new shoes or other things we needed. We knew Amá could not give them to us. Once, when we finally did catch up with him, he showed us a happy face and took us to eat and listened to us recite all our needs. When we were through eating, we all shoved away from the table as he searched through his pockets, pulled out some change, and handed it over to us. "Here's money for candy. Tomorrow meet me at Tía's house and I'll give you the money for the shoes you want."

We ran home anxious for tomorrow to come. Amá asked us, "Did your *papá* give you the money?" "No," we answered, "he said for us to meet him at Tía's house and he would give it to us." Amá warned us, "Why trust him when you know what he's like?" This still meant nothing to us. We began counting the hours until we would meet him. In our minds we would go over and over this meeting, when and where it would occur. But when the hour came and we appeared, my *tía* reported, "He just left."

Estella and I followed him, as we had before, to the trashiest part of the barrio, down behind the market, behind the food stands and the street vendors to the street of bars. It needed no address; it was announced by the dark smell of generations of lost souls.

Repulsive odors arose from the ground and the walls. To the people outside, the street of bars was enclosed in darkness. It seemed like a curse was cast upon this street, slowly transforming everything in it into trash. Men lay in doorways with dry vomit in their mouths. There were young ranch girls who were known by housewives of the town as *"decertoras del metate, mujeres resuscitadas que vienen muy mansitas del rancho y después sacan las uñas"* ("floozies who come from the ranches shy and timid but who later put out their claws"). They stood squeezed into their tight dresses with half their breasts exposed, looking like stuffed sweet potatoes. The drunken men, pants hanging halfway down their backsides, played with their breasts. Musicians strolled from one end of the street to the other, hoping to make their quota for the night.

This time the swinging doors of the cantina opened and a pair of drunks came flying out, landing heavily on the ground in front of us, one bleeding from the mouth, the other with one black eye. Estella and I stood beside the door looking for somebody safe whom we could ask, "Can you call my *papá*, Fidencio?" When someone finally did get him to come out, he said, "What are you doing here?" And we told him, "You told us to meet you at Tía's and you would buy us shoes. Since you weren't there we came looking for you." Then he couldn't get the *centavos* out of his pocket fast enough, so anxious was he for us to leave that place. And still we continued to follow him.

MOTHER'S DAY was a holiday that provided an excuse for the men to declare their adoration of their *madres* through a fog of tequila. Mother's Day dawned with no need of crowing roosters or ringing church bells—the loving sons had already started their bottles of tequila Saturday evening at the cantinas. As the night progressed and the serenading continued, music came from all directions, trumpets, guitars, clarinets playing the songs of the homeland. Slobbering poets held forth on every street, and a multitude of scents rose from carts lining the streets of town and filled with red, white, and yellow flowers—flowers to be bought for the *madrecitas* on their day. But for the mothers of their own children it was a different story.

On the night before Mother's Day, Apá had made a promise to Estella that he would take her birthday shopping. She was to wait for him at his house. She arrived and waited, waited until her small eyes finally closed and she fell asleep. She was awakened suddenly by the loud music of the mariachis. She looked out the window, but it was dark now and she couldn't recognize the faces in the crowd of men climbing out of an old flatbed truck. At first she thought it was Don Pancho coming home from work to serenade his wife, Doña Erlinda. But no, as they got to the house she recognized Apá staggering up the sidewalk with a prostitute. Behind him was another drunk with his woman. They held onto each other, dancing and stumbling up to the house. The musicians followed them inside. Estella panicked. She couldn't leave because they were all in the doorway. She ran from room to room, eventually hiding under the bed hoping they would leave—but they didn't leave.

Although the old truck rumbled down the street, now voices approached the room. She slid out from under the bed and ran to the closet, curling herself into a ball, terrified of being found. She could hear the giggles of the women, the loud breathing of Apá, the noises of the bedsprings. Suddenly her fear overcame her. She rushed out of the closet, out of the house, and ran trembling to the neighbors. When asked what was wrong, she was too embarrassed to tell.

Apá tried talking to her, but she could no longer look him in the face. She now saw him for a liar, cold and insensitive. He knew that the Mother's Day orgy happened every year, and that shopping with his child would have been totally out of character for him on that particular afternoon. But in spite of knowing, he had misled her, promising her something he knew he could not deliver. Estella never again trusted him or went in search of him. She buried him just as Mary had. As for myself, it took much longer, but like them, I too eventually buried him.

Wailing Cry

~

It was actually better for us that Apá didn't want to leave his country. Maybe he actually considered us for once, knowing that he couldn't live up to the commitment. In any case, we no longer had to be afraid of Apá coming over and hurting Amá when he found her alone. This decision also put an end to his attempts to reconcile with her. Over and over again, he had tried to tell her that he was going to change, while he still continued his wild nights. Each time we went looking for him we found him with a different woman. Amá would hear about Apá's adventures either from us or from neighbors.

One afternoon Apá had come around, expecting us to be in school, but it was a holiday and we four girls were playing out in the street when he arrived. We didn't know he was home, so when I ran inside the house, I was surprised to see him in the kitchen. He was kneeling down in front of Amá begging her forgiveness. He swore he wasn't going to hurt her anymore in any way, and that he wanted his family together again. Amá told him that he wasn't hurting her, but he was hurting his children. Amá kept repeating, "No, Fidencio, no."

In his rage, he threw a glass of water at her. Then, to make a bigger impression on her, he grabbed a picture of Amá's favorite patron saint and put it right in front of her face. He had placed it so close to her face that she couldn't move without hitting it with her face. Amá turned pale with anxiety. Next thing, he smashed the picture onto her face. I felt my heart drop to my feet with fear. I yelled for my sisters, but they were already there. I looked at Amá, and I saw the pieces of glass drop to the floor. Blood ran from her face down to her feet.

Without communicating, my sisters and I attacked Apá.

Mary grabbed Apá by his curly hair, and my sister Estella climbed on a wooden crate so she could hit my father on the head with a cast-iron skillet. I ran as fast as I could to our nearest neighbors. I ran into their kitchen without even knocking. The woman was washing dishes when I charged up to her with a lump in my throat. I was so frightened and breathless I couldn't even speak. After a few moments of trying, I grabbed her by her apron and told her to go to my house because my *apá* was hurting my mother. By the time we got there, another neighbor was already there. Disgusted, the two women told Apá to leave or they would call the police. Without even turning to see if Amá was all right, Apá was out the door. My sisters and I were in a state of utter terror. I remember being choked by this emotion. My whole body was tense and stiff with fear.

Later, Joe returned home. The house was unusually quiet. Everybody was too afraid to talk about what had happened. Joe asked what was wrong, but nobody answered. He saw Amá's face. He became enraged. His eyes burned with anger so intense I felt that if he had stared at an object it would have burst into flames. He told us to call him at work if Apá ever came over again, whether Amá agreed or not. For many days after that incident, I was full of terror, partly because I thought God would punish me for wishing Apá's death.

How, I wondered, could a man who abused his family in so many ways engage in religious acts? Yet I had seen Apá perform his ceremonial rituals. Many times I had seen him walking on his knees from the *litero* ("courtyard") to the altar to pay a *manda*, the price of a favor from God or one of the saints. When he was finished his knees would be bleeding. This was like making a pact with them for doing a miracle in response to his request. One pays a *manda* with some kind of self-sacrifice. My father carried on these rituals from the old days.

When I was just a little girl, four or five years old, I remember my uncles and my father going off into a room. It was a time when no one would talk about what was going on in the house. Everything was very secretive and unspoken. We sensed that there was a mystery going on, so my sister Estella and I stood outside the doorway and stealthily peeked in.

When they all came out of the room, it was hard to distinguish one uncle from the other. My *apá* and *tíos* resembled frightening evil animals, their faces painted with sharp red and white stripes. Their bare chests were bleeding red, as if they had been in a bullfight. Their lower bodies were covered only with muslin loincloths. Their ankles were wrapped with *cascabeles*, which kept the beat of the rhythm as they stomped. The *penachos* ("feather headbands") they wore made them appear more ominous. The shiny red-and-green material of their capes gave us the feeling they could indeed swoop down and take us away with them.

Not wishing to be recognized, they all left the house immediately. Later, Amá took us to where they were congregated. Around us we observed a small gathering of people of all ages and all kinds, which was soon to grow and consume the whole *litero*. A silent energy seemed to hypnotize and engulf the people of the crowd. We children stood in the shadows and watched the figures gyrate in billows of dark black smoke. We thought then that the smoke of the bonfire, smelling horribly of burning hair, seemed to have the power to suck people into another world, leaving their brainless bodies behind. To them it was a rite of purification to drive out evil spirits.

The men were howling and chanting, and we feared that they were turning into wolves! Sounds of the *teponazli* drum and the clay flute accompanied the cries, which were considered sacred. When suddenly the spell was broken, stillness set in. Then the Danzante, dressed as a devil, burst from the ground snapping his whip. He hopped with both legs together and landed in front of us, pushing his devilish face as close to us as he could. Before we could catch our breath he returned to the circle, departing as quickly as he had appeared, leaving us petrified.

These diabolical rituals were performed in honor of Saints Day, or when a member of the Danzantes died. The celebration could last anywhere from one to eight days. At that age I didn't understand if these acts were good or bad. It certainly hadn't stopped Apá from snapping and turning on us like a rabid animal whenever life's little inconveniences appeared. Misplacing his hat was still an event significant enough to warrant a beating for Amá.

Domingo
~

Domingo, Sunday, was a family time, a festive day for everyone. We would gather at Abuelita's house because she was the most important woman in the family. On Sunday, Abuelita was a queen; she could do no wrong. Her only function was to give orders, and whatever she desired was provided, from a bottle of tequila to mariachis. She would sit in the middle of her living room in her rattan chair, surrounded by all her "friends," her statues of the saints. Some were facing the wall, being punished for not honoring her petitions. She considered this room to be her throne room, and we all lined up, from the youngest to the oldest, and took our turn kneeling in front of her and kissing her hands. When she blessed us, her pure, dark face almost resembled la Virgen de Guadalupe. She shut her eyes and crossed our heads with her finger as she appealed to Jesús, María, y José. I believed she was the only one with the power to speak to Jesus.

On this day, the *tías* would gather in the kitchen and confide in each other about the abuses suffered at the hands of their husbands during the week. The women were tired of listening to my *tíos* and my *apá* boast about all the things they had, or had had, or would soon have. The women knew nothing would change. After greeting Abuelita they would crowd into the kitchen and take out their frustrations on the food they were cooking, smashing their foolish husbands' brains out as they pounded the dough, then burying them a thousand times in hot chiles.

Occasionally I would overhear an aunt saying she wished she had the nerve to mix rat poison in the tortillas. "And all their intestines would be burned," she'd gloat, as she furiously pounded the dough. Another *tía*, peeling red roasted chiles, would agree, "That would be good indeed. The chiles would burn all the way to the end." Then from another corner, "Quiet, they'll hear us."

And the men—I wondered how the men could turn on and off so fast. They were like chameleons, changing from one personality to another from moment to moment. Their moment of adoration of Abuelita in this culture of matriarchy filled them with gentleness and esteem that was felt around the room. It was as if a diamond illuminated the faces of everyone present. But within a split second the beautiful diamond would turn into a burning, black piece of coal.

If a *tía* approached her husband, urging him to go home because he was too drunk to stand, he would show a cruel disinterest, with a shrug and a look of revulsion that one might give a beggar on the street. Then our aunt's face would turn dark with fear and rigid as stone, waiting to see if she would be hit or not. How confusing it was to be a child! We had within us a part of the Abuelita who was being adored, a part of the *tía* who was being threatened, and a part of the abusive chameleon—with no idea how to separate them.

The Domingos always ended with someone crying. When we were younger we loved going in spite of it all. It wasn't the food or the gossip that kept us anticipating Sundays. It was the Sunday peso we received every week from our uncles. As we got older we understood better that the pesos had a price. Before giving us the coin, my uncles performed a ritual that hurt us very much. They would pick out the most obvious flaw in each of us and assign a nickname based on it. We could not dare cry or show emotion, because this would encourage them to continue the harassment for the entire day, and even carry it into the next week if they felt it was effectively humiliating.

My dark skin gave them much cruel pleasure. They would gather in a circle in the backyard with their pants undone, resting after their meal and drinking more beer. When I came around to ask for the Domingo peso, they would tell me to take a bath to wash the black off to make myself white. They would tease me by telling me that I had a disease and was not to come near them. The uncles would not leave us alone until they saw the tears rolling down our cheeks. Then they would say, "*Más fuerte, muchacha.*" ("Cry louder, girl.")

Meanwhile, Abuelita wanted us to go across the street and refill her Coca-Cola bottle with "medicine." This was what she called it, and we didn't know any better, except that it made her happy after she took it, and she pranced around the room and then fell asleep. Our *tíos* swore they would give us a belting if we did. Thus deprived, Abuelita became hostile, her eyes livid. She would leap up from her rattan throne and chase us around like chickens. She would spread her legs and hunch her back, her arms raised to each side and her hands wildly waving in the air. Shuffling her body from side to side, turning around and around in tight circles, she would frantically start cursing and at the same time make the sign of the cross, as if to defend herself from demons.

"Abuelita, what are you doing? Why are you so mad?"

"*Si no me hacen caso, le voy decir al chamuco que se las llevan con el!*" she would reply. ("If you don't listen to me, I'm going to tell the devil to take you with him!") She would conjure up the image of *chamuco*, a male cadaver covered with thick strands of hair on fire. His red eyes were grotesque like a tumor and beat like a heart. We thought he could snatch us away with his enormous wings and curling claws, and drop us down into everlasting pits of fire. She mumbled on, "*Estoy haciendo que el maldito chamuco se salga de aquí.*" ("I am making the devil get out of here.") While she was still carrying on, we fled as fast as our legs could run.

A particular domingo stands out in my mind. We met at Abuelita's house at the usual time. It was always before lunchtime; we started off early because Amá liked to lend a hand with the cooking. Everything had to be fresh and made from scratch. As always, on this day my Tío Juan was finishing the slaughter of the goat. This event brought many uninvited guests, especially dogs. They looked like they had just been released from a concentration camp and were going berserk over the smell of fresh meat. So were the flies circling the carcass, but none of this seemed to bother my uncle. He was busy draining the blood out of the headless goat, collecting it in a tub. We approached him and he stopped what he was doing when he saw us. His hands were covered in blood. He held the butcher's knife in one hand and extended the other for us to kiss.

Mary looked straight into my mother's eyes with anger and revulsion. She said, "You don't expect us to kiss his hands!" Amá answered, "Where is your respect, *muchacha*?" Mary said, "I will kiss his hands only if he washes them first. Better yet, I'll never kiss his dirty hands again. Neither will my little sisters!" She didn't stop there. Ideas had been festering in her mind for a long time. She blurted out what she thought of the *tíos*—they were liars and hypocrites and did not deserve respect. In shock, Amá warned her that the devil was going to appear and would get her for talking about her uncles that way. Mary said, "Fine. Here I am." And that was the end of the Domingos for us.

From then on we became no good to them. We were to become *mujeres perdidas* ("lost women") in their world. It was believed that not having a man in the house would mean that the women and children of the family were no good. Now we had proved it by not being submissive, by being ungrateful. At the time we weren't thinking of the twenty years to come. We thought only about not having to kiss those dirty hands. Mary's confrontation made our uncles leave us alone. Amá pleaded with us to return to the family and apologize for our rudeness. She was very embarrassed that her children had not been polite to her brothers-in-law, but we refused. In the end, they still brought us groceries once in a while, but Amá made excuses for not visiting Abuelita anymore.

Mujeres
~

What kept the women from openly expressing the feelings that rattled their hearts? We were only allowed to talk about good things or everyday events. I remember one middle-aged woman who walked about holding her two children's hands, with her gaze directed always to the ground. One morning I heard her sobbing through the vines as we harvested the grapes. Then I heard her husband scold her, asking what good was it to cry. A couple of days later when we overheard Amá and Doña Teresa talking about it, we learned that she had had a miscarriage. Why was the woman not allowed to cry?

Sometimes out of an entire family, just one member would be picked up by la Migra and taken away. The mother could not express her concern for her son because the father would say, "Do you think by crying they'll bring your son back?" The same was said when the women received bad news about sickness or death in the family. It didn't matter if it was the person closest to her heart—she should not cry, she should not spend her energy weeping, it was a waste of time.

In this camp so far from home, unwelcome memories, long forgotten, entered my brain. I recalled on certain dark, humid nights Amá would drag us out of the house, half asleep, because she had reason to believe that Apá might bring his party woman home. We would finish awakening as we passed the *casa de las tortillas*, which we tried to sneak past without capturing the attention of *las viejas tortilleras*, whose job was to attend the tortilla machine and catch the tortillas before they landed on the dirt floor. Clustered in the window, minding everyone else's business, they would shout so we could hear, "Doña Elisa, where are you going so early with those girls?" Amá let the question fly by; yet still indignant, she sarcastically mumbled, "They are like those women who work for the newspaper." At least she could see a glimmer of humor in this intolerable situation. As for us, we ended up at an uncle's house.

At times, when the women were together, stories were shared and tears were shed, but people didn't allow much time for sorrow. Before the first tear was dried, a song was in the air. The sadness of the poor was quickly dealt with the only way we knew how, by singing. People sang about things they couldn't talk about, and the songs all said, *"Tienes que olvidar"* ("You must forget").

However, one very hot and dry Sunday I cannot forget, and somehow this song reminded me of it. I was quite small, and we were living in Apá's house in Mexicali. Amá had followed the impulses of her heart by making the house look perfect, as if a king were coming to pay us a visit. She had started early in the day, moving beds, having us wash down the walls. Nothing seemed to please her the way it was. She wanted everything changed. She moved the lamps from place to place. She had us dust her knickknacks until they shone like jewels. They were collected during her years of marriage and her travels. She had a story for each of them.

Nothing she had would have cost more than a dollar or so, but she was so proud of them. She had a family of white poodles that were attached by a little chain, papa poodle to mama poodle to baby poodle. She had a white-and-black china cow. My favorite of all was a little black baby doll. It had different diaper colors and a pigtail that stood straight up on top of its head. Although it could only have cost ten cents, she wouldn't allow us to touch it. She also had two untouchable, fat dolls, three feet tall, that had dimples on their hands. They stood by the end of the bed with their big blue marble eyes, looking like two children who had been grounded for hours, just staring at the wall.

Yes, Apá was expected, and she wanted the inside and the outside of the house sparkling clean for his eyes. On her knees she scrubbed the red cement patio floor. We helped by bringing buckets of water to rinse it. Her body was dripping with sweat. She worked nonstop, scraping until the color of the floor was shining through, and then she gave it a final wiping with kerosene. This was her way of waxing the floor.

She left the most beautiful detail for last, dressing up her bedroom with delicate purple satin curtains that matched the ruffle bedspread. We knew she was anticipating an important night. She acted nervous, and had her hair up in pin curls hidden under her scarf. The evening was young when she sent us to bed. As it was too early to fall asleep, we begged her to let us stay up. Then she gave us that look and we ran to our beds.

From our room we could see her reflection in her bedroom mirror. First she gently removed the hairpins, separating each strand of curls one by one as if each was made of silk. She cared for each curl in the same way until she had completed the delicate operation of arranging her hair. She opened a pancake stick and smeared a couple of streaks on her face. As she moved closer to the mirror, it looked to us like she was finger-painting her face. Blending with an upward stroke, she applied it evenly on her skin, working down toward her neck, caressing herself to a soft, healthy glow.

I thought she already was beautiful, but tonight she needed everything, like the house, to be perfect. As she gave her make-up the final touch of a powder puff, she closed her eyes for a moment and slipped into a dream. The image in the mirror was that of a radiant woman, satisfied, savoring a luscious moment. Lightly, she fluttered the powder puff down her shoulders, her chest and back, enhancing her bronzed glow. I loved watching her outline and accentuate her slim, small lips. The dark, berry red lipstick made her look vibrant and alive. I watched as she pinched her cheeks, then moistened her finger with her tongue and smoothed her eyebrows.

She turned from the mirror and briefly disappeared from view. We lost her for a few minutes before she returned for a final glance of approval. Thinking she was alone in the intimacy of her bedroom, she admired herself in her white floral dress with the neckline that revealed not too much, but just enough, of the soft, womanly flesh of her breast. She couldn't help but feel beautiful. The bodice of the dress was closely fitted, with shoulder pads that emphasized the strength of her shoulders. The flow of the full skirt made her move like a butterfly.

This was someone else—not our Amá. She was beautiful. We never saw her dressed like this. We always saw her covered from head to toe in oversized work clothes. In a few minutes she had become daring. On went a long-sleeved bolero, covering the bare arms. She sat on the edge of her bed, and the dress flowed around her while she pulled on her favorite colored silk stockings. The seams curved with the muscle of her calves when she slipped on a pair of high-heeled shoes. She looked to us like a queen, waiting for her king.

This was the picture in my head when I went to sleep. This and the calm from the light of the little candle that Amá had sitting on our nightstand, and the comfortable night sounds of frogs and crickets. Our hearts were filled with pleasure because of our mother's beauty, and her joy in it.

Suddenly we were awakened by the shrill voices of two terrified women. I don't remember how we managed to get from our beds to where they were. Hysteria took hold of us all when we saw my father handing a gun to an unknown woman and saying to her, "Shoot her now." Shocked that Apá would ever ask her to do such a thing, the woman threw the gun back at him and started running away. Instantly I closed my eyes, afraid of what was going to happen. After the gun went off, I opened them. Apá had fired it; the bullet had grazed my mother's temple. Seeing us, she collected herself. This too we had to forget. This happened to be Mother's Day.

Hanging on Lisa's wall is an oil portrait of us, the perfect, wholesome family. In a corner of the picture there is a hole where the bullet went through the mat. It serves as a reminder of what life can sometimes be. Amá said it was not important and that we must forget it ever happened.

It took me many years to reach the point where I could express the sadness and pain in my heart. I felt safest by keeping it secret. Amá said it was all right to dream and make lots of plans, because dreams and plans cost no money. We did lots of that. My biggest dream was for this way of life to one day end.

Amá was so preoccupied with survival that she had no time to think, or to see that the darkest nightmares we experienced were lived in our own home. We heard many family secrets, secrets of people we knew here and ones we didn't know in Mexico. It was here I became aware of the painful truth of my own heritage, and here the idea was reinforced in my mind that all *padres* were the same. They were what a father was supposed to be. My eight *tíos* were the closest things I had to a father, and they treated my aunts the same way. Every morning, the women awoke wondering how to deal with the men's moods, studying how to keep them happy to ward off a beating.

We often spent weekends at the house of one of my aunts. It was full of laughter, and we really enjoyed being there. Tía laughed with us. Everything was fine until my *tío* got home. We could hear his heavy footsteps approaching, and we would immediately hush as if we had done something wrong. His presence hung in the room, and a feeling of sudden disaster came over us. Even though Tía always catered to his mood, it did not seem to matter. Something would always go wrong. While we ate breakfast, she ran around like a nervous maid, tripping over her feet trying to serve all twelve of us at once. Suddenly, Tío might pop off his chair and grab my aunt by her hair.

As I watched this I rebelled against Amá's words "Always respect your elders and life will go better for you." I was filled with emotions of both love and hate for my aunt as she covered her head in anticipation of the next blow, never protesting, never fighting back. Being so young, I didn't understand who was the stronger. I just knew it was unfair that we had to be saddled with all the destruction he caused. In a couple of seconds it looked like a cyclone had passed through the room. He had slammed chairs upside down on the floor, broken dishes, and smeared food on the floor. Tía was slammed against the wall, then thrown down on the concrete floor. She begged to not be hit anymore as she lay there looking like a defeated animal. The ten of us gathered like frightened little mice, too scared to move. In my mind and with all my heart, my hate urged her to retaliate and defend her dignity.

My aunt never questioned him about the beatings for fear of her life, but I longed to. I wanted to know what justified his behavior. We weren't allowed to question or talk about such occurrences. Perhaps the tortilla wasn't warm enough for him, or she didn't put enough salt in the beans. We would be scared and packed together in the corner. The boys couldn't interfere, because if they did the situation would become worse. Then they would end up being kicked in the rear or in the head. It was so painful to see my aunt cry. It didn't make any difference to Tío, as long as he was able to make his point of who was the head of the house.

We could tell when our uncle had been with other women. The collar of his stiff white shirt would bear traces of red lipstick when he got home. We never talked about his frequent, even nightly disappearances, but we all knew what was going on. If Tía remained silent, he might come home with a generous heart and give us each pocket change. But if she questioned or accused him, the entire household would become a hellish place before he disappeared again.

I saw all women as mothers. I felt safe in their presence. They were round and soft and beautiful, and there was no problem they couldn't solve. But the men saw them as worn-out hags they yelled orders to. They were not allowed to steal time for a nap or any other comfort. At times I would hear the husbands say to them, "You look like a dog." There was in fact a commonality among them, each developing the same etched face, which mirrored the same story. Their husbands had forgotten that when they first met, their wives were as beautiful as fresh roses. They made promises to love and cherish them, but instead they took the bloom of youth and wilted it with the lashes of their tongues and the blows of their hands. They then stupidly wondered why their women walked through their days looking so numb, their faces set like stone.

A woman's appearance became the least of her worries as the demands of her workload claimed all her energy and time. The passage of time did not favor these women who aged early. Their once iridescent, blue-black hair, now matted and greasy, was hidden under a scarf or a rebozo. Their weathered and lined faces were maps of their despair. Their beauty faded and changed like the leaves on a cold tree in winter. They traded their youth and beauty for wayward husbands and too many children.

As I reach back in my mind and take from my store of painful memories, this has to be the most monstrous yet—a day we were in Apá's way. I must have been about nine years old. Apá brought home a strange woman whose face was painted up like a clown's. It was the dead of night, early morning, when they arrived and he ordered Amá to take her children and leave the house. Amá refused. There was no place she could go. Apá grew enraged. He grabbed up the long kitchen knife that seemed to appear from nowhere and threw it at Amá. It landed in her right breast, making a large wound and leaving her in a bath of blood. It was so horrible! The dripping blood poured from her breast and pooled at her feet.

We all did what we were told to do—forget, just like all of the other times we were told, "*Tienes que olvidar.*" So we tried to block out the horror. As I grew older, and the scar would catch my eyes, it gave me the eerie feeling of reliving a nightmarish scene. I would turn my face away from the scar, not wanting to remember what happened there. I never failed to get the same feeling of being sick and afraid. I shudder when this memory resurfaces.

The mind is as mysterious as the ocean that holds hidden treasures deep on the bottom, like a locked chest that's lost in the ocean for hundreds of years, battered by the elements and buried. Surprising itself, a memory rises to the surface, sweeping to shore. It opens itself, releasing the treasures or tragedies. Eventually, they all come to light.

Part Two
~

Bleach

~

It was supposed to be the greatest summer ever, because we would spend it away from home. Amá sent us to stay with my favorite aunt, Tía Flora, in Tijuana. We all loved her. She retained the youthful smile of a little girl in a round and pudgy face. Only her wavy salt-and-pepper hair revealed her true age. The style itself never changed. Her hair was always swept back and twisted neatly at the sides of her face.

My Tía Flora's voice was soft even when she was angry. When we did not listen to her, she would threaten to tell our father, but she never followed through with her threat. Her day was fully occupied with housework and caring for her eight children, who were all twice her size. She had a generous heart and did not distinguish between her own children and us. We were excited to spend the summer in their new, almost completed home.

And then there was Ramona. . . . Aaah! She was the oldest, most voluptuous cousin in the family. Ramona exuded a smoky sensuality that seemed to roll off her in waves. Her beautiful long, thick, golden brown hair covered her wide backside and swung from side to side with the rhythm of her hips. Her eyes were light and appeared to have streams of gold surrounding the pupils. Her breasts were big and looked very heavy. She would cut the pointy tips off her long-line bra, exposing her silver-dollar-sized nipples through her sheer blouse. I asked her one time, "Ramona, why do you do that?" She answered, "For ventilation." Men's eyes followed her as she worked her way through the market. Ramona was very much like a coral snake, beautiful to view but deadly to touch. She could cut to the bone with her harsh words, then laugh them off as a joke.

One unbearably hot afternoon, Ramona's ventilated bra wasn't relief enough, and she wanted to cool off by taking a bath. She hollered out from in front of the house, calling for me to come and prepare the bathwater. Accustomed to taking orders from her, I didn't even think twice about it. As I began running up the hill toward the house, I heard her continue, "Next, after you finish that, put yourself in bleach, so you can peel the black off." My cousins and neighbors playing nearby all heard it. They were laughing and repeating to me to take a bath in bleach so I would get white, parroting what came out of Ramona's obnoxious mouth.

Their taunting transformed me with rage. Did they not know how hard I scrubbed and scrubbed my skin with the *estropajo* ("rope scrub")? But the color would not come off. I reached the house where my *tía*, as usual, was in the kitchen cooking. That day she was working the flour tortilla dough, sweat beading on her forehead. She looked preoccupied, but with "eyes in the back of her head," she asked why I needed the water. I told her Ramona wanted me to prepare a bath. Tía glanced my way and said, "Be careful, don't burn your-self." I got the bucket, filled it from a cement tank outside, returned to the kitchen, and placed it on the stove to heat. When the water was ready, I carried it outside to the little room next to the house. I dumped the water in the tin bathtub, mixing it with cold. I tested it to see if it was comfortable. Yes, it was comfortable.

The bleach was not hard to find—it was just a few steps from the bathroom. Picking up the bottle, I asked myself, "Should I or shouldn't I?" I unscrewed the cap and poured the whole bottle into the bathtub. "Should" won.

Holding the empty bottle in my hands, I realized what I had done. My eyes popped as I looked into the water, trying to fan the fumes with a towel. I opened the curtains that served as a door. The room was roofless and the odor of bleach quickly evaporated into the air. I must have done a good job because my cousin Ramona sang all the way through her bath. And afterwards, believe it or not, her skin color was just like mine. The only thing white was the whites of her eyes. She suffered second-degree burns, and to this day, it is me she remembers the most of all her relatives.

Abuelita

~

My abuelita, *Doña Demetria*, was a character. She dressed herself like an old *guerrilla de la revolución de Pancho Villa*. She looked like someone out of the past in her long, colorful gathered skirts, with her rebozo crossed in front and back as if she were carrying a machine gun. Her two thick braids hung over the front of her shoulders. She talked only of the past and treated my *tíos* as if they were still children.

Abuelita had her days turned around. Days were nights and nights were days, and there was no convincing her otherwise. Her biggest concern was how to manipulate one of her sons to bring booze to her. After she was good and drunk, she entertained whoever was taking care of her by putting on a show. She pinched both sides of her skirt and twirled and waltzed herself around like a drunken butterfly. When Abuelita's energy ran out, she would crash on the floor where she was.

My *abuelita* was a feminist before anybody ever heard of the word. She was gutsy, crazy, and demanding. I often heard Abuelita referred to as a witch, probably because of a certain look she had when she didn't want people around. She would raise one eyebrow, which gave her a mean, evil look. She twisted her lip to the other side. But I never saw her do anything abnormal except talk to the walls.

The first time I saw her doing this, I thought she talked to saints in the wall like Amá did. Sometimes she spoke in a friendly tone. Other times, I heard her chasing something or saw her madly shooting at the air as if she was trying to kill flies buzzing around the small room. I would come in and ask, "Abuelita, who are you talking to?" And she would answer, "Can't you see them? My spirit friends? Who else would I be talking to?" I looked around to where she pointed, but I saw nothing. I figured if she said they were there, they were there.

For quite a while Abuelita had an obsession with *la muerta que viene en forma de mujer* ("the dead that come in the form of a woman"). She claimed *la muerta* wanted to take her away. Her eyes followed the invisible spirits and she'd say, "Go away!" I guess Abuelita was right because they soon came for her.

Amá took us out of school to pay our respects to Abuelita during her last days. Before we got to the ranch, we made a stop at a clothing store and bought a soft lavender dress. When we arrived at the ranch everything seemed normal. There was the ever-present smell of the sewer water from the canal and the multitude of flies and mosquitoes, pesky as usual. Not too many relatives had come yet. There were a couple of aunts busy in the kitchen preparing big pots of chocolate and baskets of *pan dulce*. Amá went to greet them and they all hugged each other. As always, we children kissed their hands. Amá then disappeared for a while to prepare Abuelita for "exhibition." She didn't let anyone follow as she closed the door behind her.

After a while, Tía Micaila came to get us so we could say good-bye to Abuelita. We didn't have any idea what to expect as we entered the small room. The atmosphere was heavy with the smoke from the candles and the sickly smell of age and decay. Amá stood stiffly, shooing the flies away from Abuelita's mouth. Estella's attention was taken up pondering what could have happened to Abuelita's thick, once-resplendent braids, now painfully thin and wispy like two little strings. In a small bed covered with pure white linens, Abuelita lay looking like a very old little girl in her new lavender dress. She looked like the saint she was not. She would never have been caught alive wearing that dress. It belied her philosophy of life. I wanted her to get up and chase all the people out of the room with her broom.

A group of women dressed in black with veils hiding their faces knelt around Abuelita, lamenting the life soon to be gone. Their eerie sounds of wailing filled the room, and they pounded their chests while reciting repetitious prayers and pleading for God and Our Lady of Guadalupe to have mercy on Abuelita's soul, creating in me the impression that death was an evil and dark place.

After the third day, Abuelita murmured a few words asking Amá to come close. In a slurred voice, she asked Amá to forgive her for all the sins she had committed against her. Amá simply said, *"Está peronada"* ("you are forgiven"). Abuelita drew her last breath, saying, "Jesús, María, y José," and sighing said, "See, death has come for me."

During those three days, in contrast to the orderly mourning of the women by the bedside, all the sons gathered outside with the tequila bottles, side by side with compadres and friends of friends. They stood around a bonfire of burning tires that sent up a deep, black smoke. More tires were added as the night wore on, the flames shooting higher as the drunken voices rose, crying and cursing, unmindful of the smell of raw sewage and burning rubber. As the crowd grew, so did the fire, until it seemed to engulf the dusty yard. The mescal and cigarettes never ran out, for there were never-ending reinforcements from the newcomers.

Before the tequila dulled their senses, they consoled each other by sharing stories. Pretty soon they were hanging onto each other and hugging as if they were all one soul, loudly professing their love and asking her not to leave—offering to give up their lives in exchange for Abuelita's. Remembering that they still had the bottle, they lifted it up and said, *"Y brindo por las madres que les dió su vida"* ("the toast for the mothers who gave them life").

With the influence of the liquor setting in, the mourning quickly deteriorated, turning into regrets and remorse and fights and recriminations for all the neglect of the past fifty years. In the frenzy of the moment, everybody fought with everybody else, literally beating each other into a pulp. The kids stumbled around with their tin cups of coffee, acting as crazy as the inebriated men. What I didn't know was that the coffee was laced with a *piquete* of booze, and that's why the women inside were soon as spicy as the men and children outside.

The people kept coming to pay their respects, but what I was interested in was a couple of women with their heads covered who had been standing long hours behind the corral. It was as if they didn't want anybody to see their faces, but I would catch them looking up once in a while. They had a forlorn look in their eyes, and their faces were deeply lined. They seemed used up in both body and spirit. Their little children hugged their mothers' legs tightly as they themselves stood meekly receiving the beating of the sun. The way they hung their heads made me sad. They seemed weighed down by the crowd's disapproval.

I grew more curious and finally asked how come those women behind the fence were unwelcome inside the yard. Each of my *tías* said the same thing: "Those women have no shame, coming over here with their bastard children. They have no respect even for the dead." Such are the rewards given to those women who become mistresses. She told me that they were the other women of my uncles, and if they came in, my Abuelita's spirit couldn't leave.

While I didn't give a second thought as to why Abuelita's spirit wouldn't be able to leave, my heart felt my *tíos'* pain. I shed tears for them as my uncles hurt over memories from their childhood. They were adults, and still they cried over the old choices made by a little bony lady who was waiting to die. She too had committed sins in the heat of passion. Life was repeating itself again in their own *bastardos*. They too had been scorned and ostracized. They had paid the price of having an adulterous mother.

As the months went by, Abuelita's absence felt like a wound that would not heal. Her influence was left behind, but it had lost its binding force. I soon regretted wasting my pity on my *tíos*. I realized that despite all they knew from their own suffering, they felt no obligation to carry on the family unit and didn't give a damn about their wives or children. They paraded around with different women, and, sadly, the family began to separate, everyone going his or her own way.

Time passed. Everybody could claim a family resemblance except me. I looked in the mirror for years and I saw only me. One day, though, I glimpsed Abuelita in my own reflection. I thought, maybe it was the style of my hair, or the fact that it was dark and curly. Or perhaps it was the same birthmark on our foreheads, or the depth of our skin color. Finally I saw a connection. Maybe I am as dark and vital as she once was!

Ragtag Band
~

My abuelita *many times* awakened to the strings of the maria-chis by her window and to the scents of flowers brought to her by her adoring sons. But I never saw my *amá* or *tías* have a *Día de las Madres* (Mother's Day) like she did. I always wondered why they were not serenaded. Was the seed of love for the wives not there?

When my father began to be public with his lover, Amá was too ashamed of what had been done to her to be seen by people who knew both of them. The celebration of Mother's Day with the in-laws came to an end.

My sister Estella, at the age of eleven, decided that Amá deserved the honor of being serenaded. She gathered together ten of us neighborhood children and transformed us into a mariachi band like no other. We didn't have beautiful suits on or big elaborate sombreros—some of us were barefooted and had dirty faces—but our instruments were special. They consisted of an old, scratched guitar with two strings, pots and pans belonging to our *amás*, a wooden spoon, a tin washtub, and several washboards. We didn't have the old rambling truck to load our equipment into, but we did have grocery carts.

Pulling and tugging our ragtag band, we ran around the neighborhood at night, crossing streets, running in the alleys, climbing on wooden crates to reach the windows. It didn't matter that we couldn't all carry the same tune or that we sang the same few lyrics over and over because that was all we knew of the song. Everything sounded good and loud. We even got help from alarmed dogs and howling cats as we entered their territory.

We gathered all our change and went across the border to buy us as many flowers as we could afford. When we reached Amá's window, we gave her flowers from the bucket we carried with us. We also handed her four sets of six glasses, all of different patterns: red little squares, white daisies, red polka dots around the rims. They were the only things that we could buy a lot of with the little bit of money we had. When our performance was done, Amá came out of her swinging door, wearing her floral muumuu, looking so surprised. She shyly accepted the glasses and the flowers, trying to hold everything in her arms, and said, "*Hijas*, this is just what I wanted," as tears trickled down her face.

Crossing the Threshold
~

Tasha was like a coin that my mother saw heads up and I saw heads down. Amá said that Tasha was a gift from God and was grateful that she lived so close by and could keep an eye on us. Amá never saw through Tasha's act as the caring next-door neighbor. I can still see her patting Amá on the back, hear her saying, "Go without worry, I'll keep an eye on the girls." Although for mother she wore a soft mask of concern, for us, when we were alone, her face turned hard.

The responsibilities this woman placed on us were enormous—everything from doing her laundry to taking care of her smallest daughter, Irma. She would blame us for her child's behavior. What hurt most were the stinging words she spoke to us and of us, telling us in front of other people that we could not do what her daughter could do because we were too poor.

The evening routine was to sit outside on the cement steps. We would hear the neighbors hollering to their friends, *"Vengas a agarrar aire fresco."* ("Come here and get some fresh air.") This was an excuse to let their tongues run and gossip about their neighbors.

While Tasha's daughter and I were playing, if one of the *señoras* noticed my dress and remarked, *"China,* that dress looks expensive," Tasha would say, "It was Irmita's but she didn't like it. Isn't she good to give you this dress?" In this way she stole any pleasure from the hand-me-downs, and when she wasn't happy with us, she would threaten to take them back altogether.

Tasha indulged her vanity during her weekly visit to the beauty parlor. She would have her eyebrows penciled in twice as big as her own, her vile red lips colored to match her toenails, which she then exposed with high-heeled shoes sporting a full-blown plastic flower.

She boasted constantly about her worldly belongings. Her mismatched pieces of scratched furniture all had stories about how they came from Los Angeles and cost her oldest daughter a lot of money. However, the only difference I could see between her house and ours was that it had a cracked and rugged bathroom, while we still had to go outdoors.

Just a few days before we left Calexico to go on a trip, the carnival was in town. There was much anticipation among the people while preparing for this great event. It was all they talked about. There were arts and crafts booths and lots of talk about what kind of stand would prove to be most profitable that year. Tasha purchased Irma's tickets for the rides two weeks before the carnival, but before the festival, the girl came down with the chicken pox.

Tasha asked if one of us could babysit Irmita the day of the carnival, and I volunteered. This meant more money for me for the rides. It wasn't hard because all I had to do was bring her things she asked for. Tasha asked me not to let her daughter scratch herself, as she would be scarred for life. Every time I saw Irmita start to scratch, I would spread cornstarch all over her body. Then I would tell her if she didn't stop scratching, she would look like that forever.

The evening of the carnival came, and my sisters were ready and waiting for me because Amá liked us to stay together at all times. Tasha still hadn't paid me for my babysitting, saying she would do so later. Off I went with my sisters, knowing we had no money for rides, but it did not matter much. We knew we would enjoy ourselves anyway.

The carnival was always held in the park. There were very few cars and many people walking. There was one blue car moving slowly along, full of cranky kids. The driver signaled me to come near. I went to the car window, and a woman in the front seat handed me a couple of books of colored tickets for the rides, saying they couldn't use the rest of them. I accepted with disbelief and was quite overjoyed. I couldn't wait to give them to Mary, as she was the one in charge. We all knew this was one of the miracles Amá always talked about.

We rode the rides, and when I climbed on the Ferris wheel, I was nearly drunk with pleasure and had half my body hanging out of the chair. I made a nuisance of myself waving to all my friends. I wanted everybody to know that we were just like them. We bought cotton candy and split it four ways. We were lost in our own private world of pleasure and left the fair at last, delightfully glutted.

It was an intolerably hot night. Some say that if you have only put a foot in Calexico, you have been to hell. When we got home, Amá was sitting in the dark by the door, fanning herself with a piece of cardboard. Our only window was wide open. As we neared Amá, we all tried to talk at once about the free tickets, so that all she heard was a confusion of sound. Finally, with a soft, tired smile she said, "God never forgets us. Now let's all go to bed."

Our bed that night was the floor. It was cooler than sleeping on the mattress. The room felt like a sauna. We slept and woke periodically with headaches and nosebleeds, our bodies wet and sticking to the floor. During the night we would be awakened by the dark shadow of Amá and feel a wet cloth being placed on our foreheads to stop the nosebleeds. She also mopped the linoleum floor to help keep the house feeling a little fresher. It had been mopped so often the design was gone.

Amá did everything possible to try and allay the heat. I now realize that she worried around the clock. As with the mopping, there was also her concern about whether the cooler was throwing out air that was too hot. She would get up every hour to hose down the padding of the vent. She said it helped the air get cooler. With all the interruptions during the night, Amá was still up and gone by four in the morning. She would work the fields and return at about two in the afternoon, take off her wet, muddy clothes, and immediately soak and wash them to be ready for the next day.

The evening after the carnival, Tasha arrived home at the usual hour. She walked into our kitchen, and I thought she was coming to pay me my babysitting money at last, but I was wrong. I heard Amá calling me and saw Tasha standing there. Now yesterday's miracle was to become today's hell.

I never got a chance to ask Amá why she was calling me. She grabbed me by my hair and twisted my body to the floor.

It felt like the roots of my hair were coming out. While I lay on the floor I looked up at Tasha, terrified, silently asking her to help me, but she just stood there making no move to help. She had heard that we were on the rides at the carnival and had come to accuse me of stealing Irmita's tickets.

Now Amá was hitting me with the thick wire ironing cord. That cord never seemed to wear out. She kept asking me to apologize to Tasha. I couldn't have even if I had wanted to because of the hold she had on me. I told her once that I hadn't stolen anything, but she couldn't hear me because she was so upset. I crossed over the pain threshold to a state of primitive rage. As I picked myself up off the floor, my stomach felt like it was being pulled upward and a horrendous feeling gripped my throat. I instantly started retching. I felt my own transformation. It was as if something invisible had filled every part of my body with hate. Innocence and trust were suddenly gone, replaced by rage. That feeling in my throat was to return again and again.

A few days later, Tasha found Irmita's carnival tickets and told my mother about them, but no one acknowledged my innocence or the injustice of my punishment. The experience left me with a wild instinct and with my guard forever up. From that moment on, I realized I had suffered a great loss. It felt as though the love for Amá was gone. The beauty I used to see in her face was no longer there. The trust was gone. I didn't care to please her in any way, and I tried to keep my distance. When she was gone for many hours, I missed her, but when she came near me I could not allow any feeling for her.

As for the neighbors, I learned to talk back to them and to say what came from my heart. It usually wasn't very polite. I had learned that it didn't make any difference. I would lose anyway, so why care? I was eight at the time, and I promised myself I would never go down without a fight.

A Neighbor's Scheme

~

There was a mysterious house in our neighborhood. It belonged to a woman who lived across the alley. It looked haunted; the drapes were always drawn. All we saw through the windows was an absurdly formed shadow lumbering slowly behind the curtains. We were curious about what lay behind those poorly hung, sun-bleached, and rust-stained curtains, which always seemed to move by themselves.

The mystery was solved one day, when we saw her standing in the half-opened door beckoning to us. We hesitated at first, and when we finally approached the door, we saw a grotesquely fat, sweating old woman wobbling on a cane. Her neck, with all its many folds of fat hanging down in front, resembled that of a turkey. We could see right away that she was half-blind too.

She asked Mary if she would like to help her clean her house. As the door opened wider, our senses were assaulted by the screech of her six cats and the smell of cat urine and feces that had soaked into the wooden floor from the newspapers. The house was overflowing with empty milk bottles, old crates, newspapers, trinkets, garbage, and piles of brittle books with pages as fragile as dried leaves. It was very difficult to know where to begin.

I tried to breathe through my mouth because the odor in that house turned my stomach. Every piece of furniture was completely covered with her collection of junk, except for one squeaky old wooden rocking chair, which sat in the middle of her living room. Her dog lay stretched out on the floor, looking more dead than alive, and as old and feeble as its owner. It smelled no different than the rest of the house. The woman told us to pick up the litter from the floor, sweep and mop it, and to wash the stacks of dirty dishes. She disappeared into her bedroom, and we began working, excited as we thought about how happy we would make Amá when we gave her this money we had earned ourselves.

We worked until late in the afternoon. Joe would be coming home from work any time, and we knew it would make him angry if we were not home when he arrived. When we finally knocked on the old woman's door to tell her we were finished, she came out and asked if we were hungry. We answered yes, and she opened a can of something, dividing it into four mismatched—but thanks to our efforts clean—bowls. The snack looked much like a treat Amá made for us when she had a little leftover money, a can of corned beef mixed with plenty of potatoes, eggs, and bacon. In the blink of an eye we ate what was on our plates and waited for the woman to pay us. Instead, she told us we should go home.

We made it back to the house before Joe arrived, with Amá coming soon after. As always, Joe asked us how we had spent our day. We told him about cleaning the old woman's house and about the snack she had given us instead of pay. I have no idea how Joe figured it out so quickly, but he was outraged that she had fed us dog food. Amá just took a deep breath and said, *"Déjenselo a Dios."* ("Leave it to God.") She told us not to go near that woman again.

School

~

Amá was right when she used to look at us and say, "How many years I wished that you girls would grow up, thinking it would make my life a lot easier. When you were small, I knew I could make you happy if I gave you a piece of candy or an old toy. But now that you are young ladies and make your own decisions, I worry a lot more!"

Amá suffered because school was the least of our priorities. We wanted to make her happy, but she didn't understand that for us, school was a waste of time. The teachers did not want the Hispanic children there, and knowing that we were unwanted, we didn't want to be there either. Amá didn't understand school grades; at the end of the year she just wanted to know if we had passed to the next level. Little did she know that our report cards showed D-minus in every subject. Teachers just promoted us because they didn't want us for another year.

The teachers often picked on the ones they thought most stupid, not recognizing the children's lack of participation and listlessness as exhaustion. Many of the ones they called lazy were working ungodly hours in the fields, trying to help their mothers avoid eviction from their homes. We all knew this, but we had too much pride to tell the teacher, for if the teacher found out, the whole school would know. We were each other's support, spending our days planning how to get back at the teachers when we got out of school. We dreamed of running them over with trucks, of putting rat poison in their coffee cups. We often told each other that when we made it big, we would come back and laugh in the teachers' faces.

I was used to one teacher or another twisting a knot in my hair and swinging me from one side of the room to the other.

I came to a point of almost welcoming the moment. I didn't go meekly—I pretended to enjoy the ride.

An obese male teacher made my friend Juana sit in the front row for no apparent reason. She had thick legs and couldn't close them together. He would ask her to read, and then his eyes would roam up her legs while his wet mouth hung open. One day she caught the dirty, bug-eyed expression on his frog face, as he was lecherously watching her legs. So while she read, she slipped her hand down under the skirt between her legs and made a gesture with her middle finger. His jaw dropped open, mouth agape, but he had to swallow her insult. What could he say to her?

I decided to teach him a lesson, so the next day I put a pack of thumbtacks on his chair. As I hoped, he sat down without looking first. He howled in pain, his face and bald head turning red with rage. He threatened to suspend us all unless the culprit was found. My friends kept their word and didn't tell, but that didn't stop him from guessing that it was me. He came toward me and suddenly yanked my hair. I thought he was going to take a piece of my scalp.

All the "rejects" of the class—children of migrant farm workers, fatherless children, and those who spoke no English—knew we did not deserve to pass at the end of the year. We hadn't learned even the basic skills to work in the factories. The teachers had this "reject" group push our desks into the hall and, day after day, had us counting the cracks in the walls and the tiles on the floor. Of course, we would just play, carefully keeping our ears tuned to the sound of a teacher's footsteps. Most of us dropped out of school because we couldn't stand the pressure of both school and home. Some who left went to work in the fields just like their parents. Others became just what their teachers had called them: "Nobodies."

For many years I felt victimized by teachers who seemed to be deaf and blind to both my language and my life. In those days, we were dismissed as unteachable because it was easier for them to make us disappear by throwing us out into the hall than to put forth the effort to help us. As for our Mexican teachers, they had their own struggles with acceptance. Every day we children were painful reminders to them of their own heritage. Like us, they didn't quite feel like they belonged.

Fresno

~

The same summer that Apá had his visa revoked, Amá heard from our neighbor Trinie about a summer job for the entire family. Mary was twelve years old, Estella ten, I was nine, and Lisa was eight. We were already used to working hard and were excited about the possibility of having a good job.

It was not unusual to see Trinie out in her yard, all fancy in her straw hat and white shirt with red polka dots. She spent hours manicuring her beautiful rose bushes and pampering her grass. Her main entertainment was minding everyone else's business. She paid attention to us only when she was sure none of her friends was around. She would often motion cunningly to Amá, as though she had a great gift for her. What she had was a big tub of clothes for Amá to press, or errands for us to run. We learned to act as if she was invisible so she couldn't trick us anymore.

Trinie's husband did not work in the fields. He had a job at the railroad station, a position with status. They had a station wagon as well as an extra car. Since we had so little, her possessions seemed extraordinary. She felt this made her superior and gave her the right to look down on us. As rich as she seemed to be, she paid Amá very little for ironing, sometimes nothing at all. Trinie thought she was pulling the wool over Amá's eyes, but she wasn't. Amá knew that Trinie shortchanged her and owed her money. Amá put it on God's "IOU" list because she was too proud to collect the money herself.

In the afternoons after finishing our daily chores, we kids had our routine. We gathered with the other children of the neighborhood to do our usual thing. At the hottest time of the day, full of eagerness, we would run up and down the alley picking through the garbage. Our bodies were sticky with sweat and dirt, and we always ended up with cuts and burns on our hands from rummaging through the scorching metal garbage cans. But it was all worth it to us. We always found that green penny that nobody had noticed, and to us it was as if we had found a dollar. The narrow alley with its dented trashcans leaning against the broken fences was like heaven to us. To our youthful eyes, these rusted old cans held treasures waiting to be discovered.

We rarely found treasure, but we did find lots of germs that gave us monstrous boils we kept passing around to each other. We got boils on our hands, elbows, knees, and sometimes under our hair, which made us go bald in spots. Our dirty necks and our boils made us the subject of jokes in the neighborhood, but it didn't stop us from searching for something new.

We tried to avoid Trinie when we were out. One afternoon we couldn't avoid her, because there she was, hollering our names like a crazy woman, sounding as if she had just lost her child. Even though we thought she was just "crying wolf," we went to see what she needed. This time it was different. She really did have something to tell. We called Amá, who came quickly, and they stood in the yard talking. We could see Trinie's mouth and hands going full speed, and we knew she was doing a number on Amá. This time, she was going to help us get rich in one summer.

She told Amá about an opportunity of a lifetime. She pumped Amá up with grandiose statements, telling her how lucky she was to have all of us kids. Trinie had heard that in Fresno, contractors were hiring whole families to work in the orchards, and they also provided room and board. She painted a glowing picture, and after listening long enough, Amá came running into the house. She had seen hope for our family, hope for a better life. Although we did not have the fare to get there, or the suitcases to carry our belongings, Amá would let no obstacle stand in her way. We were going to Fresno for the summer, even with only pennies to spend.

Amá borrowed bus fare and bought each of us a woven plastic bag to put our possessions in. Then things happened quickly. When Joe got home from work, my mother was anxiously waiting to tell him. The news didn't sit well with him. He gave her a firm look and said, "You can't do this to the girls. Did you forget what it was like before? The hard times we had when we slept outside because they ran out of shacks to sleep in?" Amá tried to respond to his words, but his voice became louder and more emphatic as he recalled other such episodes. Amá remained determined, as always. Finally she said, "Where there's a will, there's a way." And that was the end of the discussion.

Trinie would take the train, using free passes she got from her husband. She was supposed to meet us at the depot when we arrived in Fresno, and she would take over from there. Mary followed Amá around, asking in her soft, concerned voice, "How can you believe this neighbor? What if she doesn't do what she says and leaves us at the Greyhound depot? She has betrayed you before. Why do you trust her now?"

Estella, Lisa, and I didn't care about the consequences. All we thought about was the trip! As we prepared to leave, we gave little thought to the supplies we would need. We took whatever we had and felt good about it. Amá was the one always thinking ahead, so she had us run across the border to get some Mexican bread. She emphasized that it was the only food we would have for the trip, so we had to make it last.

At the bus depot, Mary and Amá stood in line waiting for their turn to buy tickets. Trinie's free passes had not come through. Amá faced the wall and pulled her handkerchief from her brassiere. Scanning the room to make sure nobody noticed what she was doing, she carefully unraveled the knot. She unfolded her pittance and handed it over to Mary. Mary was my mother's voice in this English-speaking country. It made me angry and embarrassed that my mother had to depend on one of us to communicate. I felt that her awkward gestures made her look different and sometimes ignorant, which I knew she was not. She and Mary counted the money over and over. When Mary reached the counter, she handed the attendant the money and told her the desired destination. As soon as she had the tickets in her hand, we ran out to give them to the bus driver.

Full of enthusiasm, we were able to capture all the sights and sounds, the drone of wheels and the smell of burning fuel. We saw the bus driver dressed in his gray uniform and sunglasses. He greeted us all but kept on about his business, unlocking the luggage compartment and delivering baggage to the passengers from his last trip. With all the excitement, we forgot to take the bread aboard with us. We placed it on top of the plastic bags, and the driver locked them in the luggage compartment.

I think now what a gentle soul he was. I saw him throw other people's bags and suitcases around, but our bags and five sombreros were the last ones he loaded and he handled them gently. I think he knew and cared which side of the tracks we were from. The bus moved, and, feeling happy as tourists, we left behind the sign that read, "Welcome to

Calexico." Even at my young age, I could feel a change of energy. The farther the bus got from town, the less I could feel the tightness that always seemed to live in my throat. I was able to breathe more easily as the mean, narrow-minded people we knew, with their gossipy tongues, were left behind. I knew they would soon find other targets.

Aboard the bus, I was so happy that Amá felt the same hunger for change as when she crossed the river leaving Mexico. I was proud that she had won a battle over her fear. Other people talked about their poverty and the hardships that went with it, but they never did anything about it. I don't know what their fears were, because things could not have been any worse for us. We had come literally to the end of the road, Calexico. If we could survive there, we could survive anywhere. Many times I heard neighbors exchanging stories of how they had no money for rent, or the electricity had been shut off, or a mother had had to abandon her child to a neighbor because she could not support herself and the child. These conversations always ended with the same phrase, *"Pues, ¿qué se va a hacer?"* ("What can we do?")

The trip went by fast, with so many things to see. It was like trying to absorb many movie scenes all playing at the same time. When we reached our destination that evening, Trinie was not there to meet us. We thought little of it, assuming that she had just missed us and would come back. We spent the time exploring the whole block. After two hours, though, we began to think that she might not have just missed us. Then four hours passed. People came and went. We were growing hungrier. We couldn't eat the bread because it had gotten squashed into crumbs. As more time went by, we became irritated and cranky. Amá, not knowing what else to do, tried to distract us by suggesting a walk. She made us all go to the restroom first. I crawled on the floor under the door to open the stall for my sisters. It cost a dime to use and that was a dime we couldn't afford to spend.

We realized we had been stranded and finally became scared. We found Amá facing the wall, hiding her face so we could not see her cry. She was wiping away her tears when we heard a raspy voice behind us. A little midget who only came up to my mother's waist had noticed Amá's tears and asked what was the matter. Amá told her that we were stranded and had no money to return home or to buy food. This little woman carried her money exactly as Amá did, so with her short, stumpy hands she pulled a bundle from her brassiere and handed Amá three silver dollars. Amá thanked her repeatedly, while we four girls kept staring until the woman asked us what we were staring at. She was wearing a waitress uniform, with white hose and white nurse's shoes. She was very top-heavy, small like a child but with adult parts, and her big, shapely lips were covered in a rose-colored lipstick. Because I had never seen a midget before, I asked, "Why are you dressed like that?" She replied, "Because I am an adult."

Again Amá and Mary went to the ticket agent. They asked if she could please relay a message to the woman who was supposed to pick us up. They described Trinie and asked the agent to let her know that we were just out for a walk and to please wait for us. We had walked so much already that Lisa and I refused to move anymore. Mary, frustrated and despairing, resorted to pushing, pulling, and dragging us by whatever part she could grab.

We finally got to a park where people were going about their business. We chose a bench and lay down for a while. Then we girls began to cry. Again, we realized we were lost and wanted to go home. Amá, to distract us, called our attention to what was going on in the park. She pointed out the old folks feeding the birds, men smoking their pipes and reading newspapers, even a lady who had put her wig on backwards. We didn't care. The only thing that caught my eye was a child smothering himself in an ice cream cone.

When it was time to resume walking, Lisa and I refused.

The soles of our plastic tennis shoes were burning the bottoms of our feet, and we were very hungry. Amá was determined to make the three silver dollars last, so she didn't spend them until late that afternoon. She bought us hot dogs and soda, which we swallowed so fast that they made no difference in our stomachs. We were still hungry. We wanted more food, and answers that Amá didn't have. We began to tell her that Joe was right, that she didn't know what she was doing. She simply repeated that God would help us.

Mary started stopping strangers in the street and asking for help. She was given directions to a certain building. She had such a hard time getting us to follow that she had to drag us by the hands. The more she dragged, the more we complained. Finally we came to a huge, smoke-stained cement building. Entering the hall, we were greeted by a stale, musty odor, like a seldom opened old trunk. We followed a flight of narrow, decayed stairs down to the basement. We walked close together now, all experiencing the same ominous feeling about this place. I could see many years of what looked like tearstains on the walls. At the bottom of the dimly lit stairs, Mary pushed open a door. Here we found the final hopelessness of many years of poverty and despair. Here in a soup line stood dark figures with dead eyes and hollow faces, some cripples without arms or legs. Some looked as if they had rolled in mud, others wore layers of tattered clothes. All moved like robots. The most frightening ones were the ones who began to move closer to us. First they glared, and then they broke into toothless grins. Amá whispered that it was not polite to stare, that these were just people down on their luck.

As we stood there, one of the women volunteers greeted us and put her arms around Lisa and me. She whispered to us that these men were not to be feared, that they were veterans of the Korean War and would not harm us. I guess she saw that we didn't understand, for she went on to explain that they had gone to serve their country. This was even harder for us to comprehend. I asked, "If they served their country, why are they so poor?" She didn't answer, but instead moved us in the direction of the food.

The volunteer instructed us to serve ourselves from the big pots of watered-down soup and said we were welcome to eat as many pieces of cut sandwiches as we wanted. There were trays and trays of peanut butter, cheese, and tuna fish sandwiches. There was plenty of thin powdered milk, too, but we chose to skip that. When we saw all this food, we forgot the feeling of not belonging here. We began to understand that these men were people like us and they had found their place. It was many years later that I learned that this old, cold, miserable place was the Salvation Army.

After we finished our meal, we needed to find our way back to the bus depot. Mary asked directions again, and to us it was a long walk back. When we finally arrived, we asked the agent once again if a woman had inquired after us. She shook her head "no." Amá's eyes were full of desperation. She dropped her head in defeat and walked back to the spot in the depot where we had started that morning. We all sat in the same chairs, throwing ourselves down and placing our heads on her lap. We had one more thing against us, as it was now dark outside. We felt dirty and empty, just like the place we were in. We had cried so much that we had no more tears left. We sat there waiting for nothing. We just surrendered ourselves to destiny.

Destiny arrived in the shape of a woman named Teresa. We heard the sound of a low, warm, friendly voice behind Amá's back. The voice belonged to a tall, slender woman. She asked Amá who or what we were waiting for. Her eyes glowed as if she had stolen a piece of sunshine. Her long, wavy hair was pulled back in a red bandana. She was dressed like a man, in jeans and denim shirt, but her instincts were those of a mother, a mother who recognized children in trouble. She had been in the bus depot several times that day and noticed us, always sitting in the same spot.

Amá told her our story and finished by saying that nobody had met us. The lady then told us about herself and the reason she was at the bus depot. She had come to pick up workers and take them to the camp she managed. The camp needed families like ours to help get the kitchen ready for a couple of hundred hungry men who worked in the grape orchards. She had to leave now, because her truck was full, but she said she would return for us in an hour. We watched her leave and, terrified that she wouldn't return, told Amá she should not have let the woman go without us. Amá said calmly, "She'll be back."

We stared unblinking at the depot door and an hour later saw her long legs come through the doorway. Were we ready to leave? Our eyes lit up like lamps as we gathered our bags and followed her to a brown station wagon parked outside. We couldn't have felt more joyous if we had found a long-lost relative.

The car ride erased all memories of the struggles we had gone through during the past two days. Teresa's green ranch house looked as if there was a big poker game going on. There were two large trucks in the driveway and a number of cars. When she opened the front door, the first thing we saw was an overwhelming number of boxes of pots and pans. Then we saw walls covered with family pictures, radiating warmth. Next came the sweet, familiar aroma of *yerba buena, canela,* and *manzanilla*—all herbal teas that Amá used to give us at night. I knew we were safe, that she was one of us.

Doña Teresa led us into the hall, Amá's stern glance taming our curiosity about the house. We dared a glance into the bedrooms and saw a bed in every room. Heaven! I had already taken in the fact that there was no father in any of the many family pictures along the walls. I felt again that emptiness in me and wondered where the father was, but I was too timid to ask.

Teresa led us to her daughter's room. We stood there in the hall like mummies, waiting for Amá to nod. She had always told us, "Never enter other people's bedrooms, because they are sacred." Doña Teresa understood; she smiled and said it was all right for us to go in because this was where we would sleep. Taking in the satin bedspread, Amá announced, "We will sleep on the floor," not wishing to abuse this hospitality.

Next morning we awakened to the warmth of sun on our faces. Lost momentarily in these new surroundings, I saw sunlight streaming through the soft, delicate shimmer of sheer curtains, bouncing off the bright satin bedspread, filling the room with its beautiful rays. I realized it wasn't a dream only when I heard a knock on the door and the same gentle voice of the day before asking if we were up and ready for breakfast.

We headed for the bathroom and couldn't believe what we found. There was a sparkling green bathtub and matching toilet, with dancing flowers on the wallpaper. In the tub, we slipped and slid on the smooth enameled finish, not at all like the cement tub we were used to at home. We searched for the clumsy, rock-hard soap we were used to at home, and instead found a small, perfumed white oval—just Dove, I later learned, but to us it could have been French soap. Washed, we went to breakfast, and afterwards helped to clean up the kitchen and carry boxes to the truck.

My unease and curiosity kept growing until, by the time the truck was loaded, an unanswered question flew out of my mouth: "Doña Teresa, where is your husband?" Smiling, she replied, "I don't need one of those." Amá overheard and I knew I was in trouble. I had asked an adult something that was none of my business.

Grapes

~

After we threw all the boxes of pots and pans in the back of the truck, we hopped in, alive with anticipation. Our trip from Doña Teresa's home to the camp was made more thrilling because we had nothing to compare it with. Driving through the outskirts of Fresno, we were bewitched by the richness of the land and the multitude of colorful fruits that covered the ground. Doña Teresa must have seen the longing in our eyes because she made a quick stop by the side of the road so we could get out and pick some peaches. She saw that we were reluctant and said with a grin, "Go for it, girls. The farmers welcome people who serve themselves." So we gathered up peaches that had fallen on the ground and stuffed them wherever we could. We could see what looked like an endless grove of fruit trees filled with peaches, nectarines, oranges, and figs— all the fruits we could rarely afford there for the picking.

It didn't take long to get to camp. When I saw it, I felt disappointed and deceived. It looked so isolated, so different from what I was familiar with. There was no immediate sense that this was where I would live for three months and learn so much. The rows of one-room, one-window shacks all looked alike. Some had glass windowpanes, others just an empty window frame. They all had one thing in common, a towel draped across the window. This was exactly like the home I had just left in Calexico. None of them had door locks, probably because no one had anything worth stealing. All of our possessions were on our backs.

I hadn't yet finished surveying the place when I heard Mary call out the number of our assigned cabin. As we opened the door, we immediately felt the sadness stored up in the four walls. The only furnishings were two double-sized steel army bunks. I felt sorry for the four worn, lumpy mattresses on the bed frames. There were traces where little buttons had once been, just rusted-out circles around holes. The empty feeling inside wouldn't last long; soon the room would be crowded with the lives of five women. The only way we could comfortably fit all of us in the room was to lie down. But no matter how tiny it was, no matter how leaky the roof was, it was better than a bus depot. It was home.

Departing from her housekeeping standards in Calexico, Amá never harassed us about cleaning the cabin. Here we were surrounded by dirt. The constant activity outside blew road dust into the room. She knew it would be impossible to keep our wooden floor clean.

Each morning at dawn, we were awakened by the smell of the old buses as they warmed up for the long drive to the grape fields. A tremendous cacophony began as the buses slowly coughed their black exhaust through the camp. Half-asleep children were hauled into the buses. Lunches were packed for everyone and loaded aboard. Women and men were both covered from head to toe in the same style of clothing, devised to keep off the scalding noonday sun.

The first thing to go on the bus was the ever-present pot of beans. Then the men would take turns dragging heavy water cans aboard. I don't know why we all rushed and shoved to get on the buses, because we took the same seats each day, some on the floor, others on the steps. We did respect each other's own little bit of territory. There was a lingering hunger for the last bit of sleep during the ride, but since our bodies were packed so tightly together, we could not help but be energized by one another. It was like being crammed into an overcrowded locker room. As we carried on our own conversations, we clearly heard all other conversations.

A guy sitting near the back of the bus would yell to someone in the front, "Hey, *hermano, hermano, pásame un cigarro!*" ("Pass me a cigarette!")

Another would interrupt, *"¡Pásame uno de tus tacos!"*("Pass me one of your tacos!")

The compadre would answer, *"Sí, pero son de huevos y de frijoles."* ("Yes, but they are with eggs and beans.")

"No la chingues, hermano, de esos me distes ayer." ("But, brother, these are the same as yesterday.")

"¡No, compadre, ayer eran de frijol y huevos!" ("No, yesterday they were beans with eggs!")

They started their mornings with vitality, alive and full of jokes, comparing their productivity the day before with each other, putting their *huevos* on the line as to who could outdo yesterday's hardest worker, who had the biggest *talegas* of all. Of course, there was always a brave macho man proclaiming that he was the fortunate one. The rest of the men replied, *"Sí, buey."* ("Sure, you big ox.")

I didn't understand why the men always talked about the strength of their bodies. I realize now that this was all they had, all they had to be proud of.

Without warning, the driver might slam on the brakes. With the squeal of the brakes in our ears and our bodies still in motion, the doors would open and a couple of lost souls would hop on. Ready to start again, we heard banging on the side of the bus and someone shouting, *"¡Espérenme, amigos!"* ("Wait for me, friends!") Red bandanas could be seen waving desperately in the air as men tramped out from behind the bushes, afraid of being left behind. They looked gaunt and needy, dressed in jagged, stained, and faded khaki pants that just hung on their frames. Their distraught expressions vanished when they entered the bus, a look of bravado instantly changing their demeanor. The other passengers on the bus became exhilarated. "The love of the hermano" released the fear and anguish they dared not show. They began hitting each other on the back and pounding each other's heads.

Their laughter was contagious. We couldn't help but laugh along with them. We didn't know the real meaning behind their laughter, or why Amá seemed so uneasy and upset. When she saw us becoming too amused by the clowning, she would grab for us and sharply fold a small piece of our skin, intentionally leaving a burning pinch. She would whisper, "That's none of your business, meddling kids."

Later we learned how she feared we were hearing and absorbing wrong things before our time. Neither sex nor body parts were seen or spoken about and were never a matter for open discussion at home. Amá would shake her head, "Those men have no shame at all." It was years later that I learned the double meaning of *huevos*.

The morning was still dark and chilly when we arrived at the fields. When the buses finally groaned to a stop, we thought the commotion was over, but in fact the din grew worse than before. Rushing out of the bus, Amá would find a secluded area where she could separate us from the men's gathering. Sometimes we would be near the irrigation ditch, other times behind the last bus. I thought she was protecting us from the cold, but I now know that was not the reason. We were surrounded by open space and coarse men with loose tongues.

Amá felt she was sacrificing our innocence by bringing us into the fields. When the women walked by, the men would drop whatever they were doing to ogle with bulging eyes. In mock-poetic fashion, they would compare a woman to food, letting her know of their craving as they slowly licked their dry lips. "*¡Mamacita, estás como dulce, como para chuparse los dedos!*" ("Little mama, you are like candy, good enough to make me lick my fingers!") Crude remarks such as these made the women's skin crawl.

I could not understand the men's attitudes. I saw them as fools and giggled thinking of how much they looked like dogs with their tongues hanging out as they followed the women around. Amá would cringe and quickly flee the scene. She always tried to distract us with conversation. I tried asking her what they said or what it meant, but she would just get mad at me. Nothing made sense. Was she shy? Was she scared of the men? Why?

While we waited for the first peek of daylight, we would see a couple of the men scavenging for broken crates and dry brush. Soon they would have a fire crackling under the pot of beans. This was a ritual that had to be carried out each day, and one of the many things that linked all of us together. Even though half the workers might be missing, the biggest concern was the large, sacred, burnt, and dented pot of perfectly cooked beans. While the frijoles were cooking, the aroma steamed into the air and mingled with the laughter. A stranger to the crowd would assume some sort of special ceremony was being performed, with all the shivering and trembling that went on as the workers tried to stay warm around the bean fire.

When the sun reached a certain point in the sky, the crowd would turn to the day's work. This began with a rush, as if we had all suddenly found gold, but all we were doing was getting the cheap grape-cutting knives and crates from the foreman standing near the bus. One group rushed to get the best knives, another to fight for the best spots in the vineyards. Families preferred to work together, feeling the need to be side by side.

Entering into the vineyards, we experienced a transformation. A particular beauty lay upon the untouched vines. Even the air felt new. The smell was sweet. This soil had everything grapes needed to grow. What I loved the most was that the fields provided an intimate world, a place where we had Amá to ourselves. Estella and I were always the first to explore the new grounds. Skipping along through the vineyards, I felt like I was being carried by the winds, flying loose and free. I never felt my feet touch the ground. My little footprints were the only indication I had ever been there.

Our job was to run up and down the rows placing the empty crates ahead of Amá and Mary. To save time, we tried to calculate where they would be needed next. We had a system. Working on opposite sides of a row, across from each other, Amá and Mary would not stop for hours. The only thing on their minds was to move as fast as possible and fill as many crates as they could. Estella and I had another job—to quickly move the filled crates to the end of the row. The hardest job we had, however, which was actually the most fun, was to crawl on our backs under the vines to reach the grapes closest to the ground. Mother had us check and recheck to make sure the vines were stripped truly bare of grapes.

From the back, Mary did not look like a girl of twelve. Her long, thick, coal-black braids were pushed up under her scarf. The oversized, rolled-up clothing made her look like an old lady. She acted like one too. Mary had started out as a child, but after she went into the fields, she became a woman. I didn't understand then that she was giving up her own childhood for the sake of ours. She endured the long, rigorous hours of work in one spot, just as Mother did, positioning herself on the ground without moving until her knees were molded into the dirt. She enforced a rigid discipline on herself, which also, paradoxically, meant freedom to her. This was her summer to have all the freedom she wanted, since Joe was not around to make her responsible for whatever we did wrong. But in reality, we had been her constant concern, around the clock. She was always in fear of where we were, and what we were doing.

When Mary saw us getting out of line, or not listening to our mother, she would give us the evil eye. Mary's glances hurt more than if she had pulled our hair. She did not allow herself any playtime. While other children were cutting out paper dolls, Mary would be cutting out sunsuits for us from the printed sacks flour came in. She was so fast at making things. I liked to watch her poke holes with a pencil through each side of the material, then lace a string through and tie knots. Instead of being grateful for all the sacrifices she made for us, we thought of her as mean and boring.

Estella and I had easy jobs compared to Amá and Mary.

Our first duty was to entertain Lisa, but this was not easy. Even at eight years old, she cried a lot and tired quickly. She constantly wanted water or to use the toilet, which meant that we were trudging up and down the fields attending to her needs. After so many dark, chilly mornings of feeling remorseful that she had to wake Lisa so early, Amá decided to leave her at home. We weren't one bit sorry, because it meant a much easier day for us. How I now wish that we had dragged Lisa along, instead of trusting in fate. She should never have been exposed to what happened.

As so many other mothers did with their children, Amá left Lisa in the tiny one-room shack with the only company being the picture of San Martín de Caballo that we carried everywhere we went. Amá said he would bless us with a job, and so he had. Lisa had her almost bald, cinnamon-headed baby doll to play with, a doll with yellow-green cat's eyes that was almost as tall as she was. Plenty of goodies were left at her side to eat during the day. And Lisa did a good job of taking care of herself, dressing and undressing her doll, talking to herself. But eventually she tired of this, and then she would do what the other children in the camp did when working mothers had left them behind. She left the shack.

They were not supposed to do this, but all they had to do to find each other was to lift the towel from the window and holler. So they all got together like a swarm of little bees looking for honey. They roamed the camp, dragging back garbage the campers had left behind, finding dented coffeepots and chipped, useless cups to play with.

Amá left for work troubled about leaving Lisa alone. She knew all the men were out in the fields, except for Doña Teresa's father. His face was heavy, with folds of thick skin that hung over his neck. His shirt was stretched across his fat belly, his pants held up with red suspenders that hung like tent wires over his vast body, and his blue feet bulged in black slippers. Breathing was a huge effort for him, and he was not seen as a threat of any kind to women because of a heart condition that made him weak.

My mother had even felt pity for him and had made a special effort when she prepared his plates to make sure he ate well. But her trust was misguided. He was really an alligator. He would come to the shack where Lisa was playing with her doll. He would talk to her and try to make himself a friend. And one day he started stroking her hair and slid his lumpy, veined hand up and down her chest. Lisa sensed danger in this behavior and ran from the room as he unzipped his pants. He taught young Lisa an awareness of danger, and she refused to stay there by herself ever again.

Exhausted from a full morning's work, knowing there was much more to be done, the families rallied between the rows for a break. Everyone was invited to share their tacos, and an impromptu party took place. It was different with us. We could never get Amá to take a break as other families did. We literally begged her to sit with us and have a little to eat. We wanted to hear her laugh, see her smile, but she had no time for such things. We knew she needed rest, we could see the color had drained from her face. She looked almost chalky, as if a clay mask covered her features.

It was hard to tell what Amá was thinking just by looking into her eyes. She seemed always to have a nostalgic air about her, perhaps for the days gone by in her motherland, in her youth. Occasionally when I heard her sigh, I asked her what she was thinking about. "So many things," she would answer, wondering if she would ever go back to her homeland. When I asked her why she would want to go back to a place where everyone was so poor, she just said I didn't understand.

Sometimes she looked like she was on the verge of collapsing, and periodically the back of her pants would be soaked in blood. I thought her body was ripping apart and her intestines were about to come out. When we called her attention to it, she would be embarrassed, but she would never tell us what it was.

Amá's physical appearance was deceiving. Such a frail structure, but such determination, propelled her through the smoldering heat on will alone. The rest of us would be delirious, and we were forced to take a break, but Amá continued to work. Once in a while, she would request a sip of water or dampen the handkerchief she wore under her sombrero. Her body was like a leafless branch, with her brown flesh tightly wrapped around her bones. Likewise, her belief was rooted in her as a tree roots to the earth. Mary worried. "How can you work this way?" And Amá answered, "Where there is a will, there is a way." If we could get her to eat at all, it was always after she had waited for us to eat first. Then she would accept the leftovers. The only thing I saw her buy for herself was a small can of V-8 juice each day.

Here in the vineyards, among the rows of grapes, we were all the same, with only two things on our minds. One was "Hurry, hurry, cut those grapes! The more grapes, the more money." The other was lunch, breaking the monotony of the day. This meant straight to the tacos without washing our hands or faces. There was no time for cleanliness; rubbing our hands with grape leaves was our substitute. It was normal for us to eat tacos with a little dirt inside. Amá said, "A little dirt never killed anybody." It wasn't just a little dirt on our hands—we were pasted with it. However, we ate well during this period, *como gente rica* ("as do the rich"), shredded beef, corn, hash brown potatoes, and even soda. I didn't realize that when Amá worked until midnight, she was earning us these treats, helping in the kitchen to start lunches, preparing dinners, cooking pounds of heavy meat, and lifting heavy pots.

We would sit in the fields with Mary and make great plans, like all the other families, spending our money even before we had seen the first paycheck. Fantasies circled from vineyard to vineyard, and that is where they stayed. We could overhear our neighbors' conversations, and most of what we heard sounded similar to our own desires. The men wanted to one day own their own homes. Some dreamed of owning a cantina in Mexico, others just wanted a car. One expressed an obligation to pay for his mother's surgery. Day after day, stories were shared. This was a time for the happy ones. Amá wasn't a talker. If she saw us carrying on, she would tell us to be quiet, warning that others would hear us. We never understood, but this privacy was important to her.

After the forty-minute lunch break, we returned to work with full stomachs, still digesting our hearty meal. The comedy continued, voices floating on the air into the afternoon. Or the performance might be interrupted suddenly by shouts. "The catcher is here!" The warning passed like wildfire through the rows. "¡La Migra, *hermano!*" The bushes began rustling in all directions at this alarm. Workers scattered everywhere, hiding behind vines, jumping into irrigation ditches, disappearing as fast as scared rabbits, the message still traveling row by row, "¡La Migra!" By the time the green van pulled up, the fields were empty. Some were caught, some escaped. The first time we saw this, it made us sad. After a while, we got used to it, because we knew the workers were cunning and would find their way back.

Toward the end of the day, Estella and I would hide the water container so that we would have the excuse to get off work. We would drag Lisa with us to the bus for more water. The careless, thoughtless bus driver always parked as far from the workers as possible, and he parked the bus facing directly into the sun. Walking all that distance, we withered. Lisa didn't make it any easier for us, because when she had had enough of walking, she would just keel over, heavy and rigid like a wooden doll. Grape leaves and dirt haloed her head, and her owl eyes glared up at Estella and me. Estella would say, "Okay, Lisa, we are going to leave you here so the ants can eat you piece by piece." Lisa would leap up and bolt the rest of the way to the bus, screaming all the way.

The driver always left the water cans in the sun, too, so that the water was unpleasantly warm. Also, sulfur had been added to keep mosquitoes from breeding in it. It tasted awful and left us with sickened stomachs. I did not know then why it was so disgusting, but now I know that the rust in the cans contaminated it. When we reached the water cans we quickly drank our fill, against Amá's warning. If she had been there, she would have made us wait until the water settled and the dead flies and bits of rust had drifted down from the surface.

After carrying water back, we returned to our work in the rows. We were always glad to see the end of a row because it meant that the day's work was almost over. We would look proudly at the many stacks of crates lined up perfectly and wait for the boss to come and punch our cards. The cards kept the record of what we had earned that week. While he did this, we studied Amá with concern and asked if we had done well. "Yes, we did well," she told us. We never were told how much money we had made, because that was not children's business. All we cared about was that we were through for the day. Gone were all thoughts of aches and pains, blisters and scorching heat. The minute we were finished, we felt the sweet taste of freedom. Climbing back on shabby buses, we would finally make our jostling, lumbering way home.

Hombres

~

In camp, all men had the same behavior. They all resembled drunken, self-indulgent Roman soldiers at a feast, demanding to be served. The servant was his wife. If he was a man, he had her doing three things at once. She had not finished bending her knees to start the kerosene stove when another order would be issued: "Hurry with the food. Bring me my beer!"

The men felt that they deserved to enjoy the pleasures of life as they sat around the bonfire. Their self-importance was so cranked up that a rooster crowing at dawn had more subtlety. Their hair was elaborately placed, their shirts unbuttoned to expose coarse chest hair, and a gold medal of our Lady of Guadalupe dangled on a chain around their necks, less to show reverence for the Mother of God than to serve all the other purposes gold serves. Their tight pants strained over their round stomachs, and the toes of their worn-down boots pointed to the sky, as though praying to the heavens. They strutted about as if they were gifts to womankind, offensively ripe with the odor of heavy cologne. They were sure they left a desirable impression as they strolled by. What would they have done had they known the true reactions of the women?

I immediately took an intense dislike to men who dressed this way. When I was a child I blamed it on their style and manner—of clothes, of speech and gesture. As I grew older, I realized that it was their egos I didn't like. These men reminded me of my *apá*. They were nothing better than lost souls, poor misbegottens who lived on the only thing they owned, false pride. They played well their ego roles—Mexican hombres—and failed in the more important roles of being a good husband and a good father. They were so consumed with pretending to be what they were not that they destroyed the great natural charisma they had been gifted with.

These men had many natural talents. Some could play the guitar and sing passionate songs with lyrics of great beauty. Others had the inspiration of true poets. Some were great clowns. They all must have missed their fathers and mothers, because that was all I heard them sing about. Some of their songs were very sad. They sang about what they had left behind. But they couldn't appreciate what they had, because they wanted what they couldn't have.

When on occasion we saw a gringo pass by with his children, one hand holding a child's hand, and the other carrying groceries, we understood that he was helping his wife. Sometimes we saw these men cooking dinner or playing with their children. I envied these children with nice fathers. But our men criticized and belittled the gringos for those very acts and qualities. They claimed such men were weak, stupid, and a disgrace to Mexico, if they happened to be Mexican. Little did they know that in the eyes of their own women, these remarks and jokes made them less than men.

What kind of men would they be if not for their cruel legacy? Men were made in a rite of passage such as the one my father and his friends passed on to their sons, initiating young boys into manhood through torture. Drunk and leering over a crackling fire, the men would heat an iron rod to red-hot and brand the boys' testicles and thighs. Crying was not allowed. Pain was given with the admonishment "Men don't cry."

So all of these one-time initiates would pitch in a nickel until they had forty-nine cents to buy cheap wine. No one bothered to wipe the rim. They just passed it around until the bottle ran out and their bodies ran out. It was funny for us to see them crawling on the ground, mumbling. No one understood what they were saying. Some of the drunks were fortunate to have wives who would drag them inside, while others were left to sleep outside on the ground.

Summer Ends

The summer in Fresno went by too fast. The fifteenth of August was here and the working season was over. The camp looked completely different now from when we first came. The trees were stripped bare, and only the skeletons of the grape vines were left. Memories were as numerous as the footprints left behind on the fields. Only the burned circles of the cooking fires were left in the camp. We watched the last of the buses and the jalopies disappear down the dusty road. A few rusty old beaters that couldn't make it back home were left along the road, but nothing went to waste. Next year these junk cars would make homes for a few families.

Just as the families had announced their arrival with children screaming and fighting amongst each another, and mothers hollering even more loudly for them to keep quiet, their departure was no different—loud and tumultuous. But the farewell was also sad. We had been like family, and now we were watching all of our "cousins" go their separate ways. We were the last to leave because we stayed to pack the kitchen equipment away.

A couple of days before the workers set out on the road home, Amá did a surprising thing. At the time we had many plans for the money we had earned, but like many of our plans, these changed. Before we knew it, she had bought a Chevy with burgundy velvet seats for Joe. We still had money for school clothes, but for us this purchase was as if we had bought a ranch. Querro, a fellow worker, offered to drive us back home to Calexico. We did not come home rich, like Trinie had promised, but we traveled by car instead of by bus.

When we arrived in Calexico, Trinie, boiling with curiosity about the car, came out to meet us. Now most people would not have the nerve to show their faces if they sent a mother and four children off on a bus to nowhere. But not Trinie. She simply explained that she learned shortly after we left that the camp was full and she had no way to get word to us. Mary just rolled her eyes and shook her head. I, too, wondered why Amá had believed a woman who cheated my mother out of her ironing money. Once again Amá's childlike faith allowed her to shrug her shoulders at the trouble Trinie caused us. *"Déjenselo a Dios."* ("Leave it up to God.") Joe, on the other hand, was disgusted and said, "God is too busy for small things like this; I will take care of it." Joe would not allow us to run Trinie's errands any longer, or wash her dirty laundry.

The car was our surprise for Joe, but as it turned out, he had a surprise for us too. He was getting married. The exuberance over the car quickly faded as the shock set in. Amá's heart became sad, and once in a while we would catch her crying and have to ask what was wrong. Her answer was the same answer we had heard before: *"Nada, hijas, todo está bien."* ("Nothing, daughters, everything is okay.") At the time we were too young to understand her sadness. Amá wanted Joe to be happy and to have his own family. She even knew he was responsible enough to make this commitment at nineteen. I didn't understand why she cried for him. Now I see that she was scared, and what saddened her was her deep sense of loss, as he became the head of his own household.

Even now, as old as I am and knowing what I know, I still don't think I could have been as giving as Joe was. The day of his wedding came. When he and his bride were ready to go on their honeymoon, we saw them both walk toward the car, which was covered with strings of paper flowers. We ran and grabbed Joe around his legs, panic-stricken, with tears rolling down our cheeks. We begged him not to go. Was he abandoning us? He looked down at us, gathered around him, and told us he would never leave us and that he would always be nearby. The fiesta ran until dawn, and the two of them came home with us.

It's sad to say, but my mother was not an exception to the stereotype of the "meddling mother-in-law." What my mother was doing for her loving son was an insult to the daughter-in-law, and what the daughter-in-law did for her husband was never good enough for his mother. There was no love lost in their relationship.

As for the black Chevy, it had a short life with Joe. A young man from the neighborhood took it for a joyride, and that was the end of it.

A couple of months after Joe's wedding, Amá came home from work one day very determined that it was time for our family to move from Billy's Apartments. By this time, we had outgrown our treasure hunts in the garbage cans in the alleys.

Part Three
~

The Clean Start
~

Amá decided we needed a change of scenery and neighborhood. From Billy's Apartments we moved to First Street, to have a clean start. Out in front of our lopsided new building stood two palm trees that reminded me of two ancient women. Even the habitat had taken on a feminine and worn-out, enduring air. I called the trees the *abuelas*, the grandmothers, tall with wilted strings of lifeless hair drooping around their faces. The bark of the palms was as fragile as the hanging skin of such women, but the trunks had strong, spreading roots that bound them to the earth. The yard was barren except for an occasional patch of green.

Amá saw that with hard work she could change this place. She would rearrange the shriveled, torn fence to mark the yard. She would grow her *mata de yerbe* to make her soothing tea, *ruda* to remedy earaches, bushels of *albaca* for stomach cramps, and *manzanilla* to help us sleep. The flowers transformed the yard into a middle-class paradise. The pink, yellow, and red *pericos* caught the attention of all passersby. I always thought that God made a mistake when the colors mixed, but Amá loved all flowers and plants and had success with them all. She even cultivated the lowly laurel, with its stigma of poverty, for these indigenous plants gave beauty to this dead valley with their many colors. The rich green leaves provided shade for the unfortunate and a pungent aroma to lift the spirits.

Like the plants in our garden, the colors inside our house were mismatched. Amá painted each room according to the donations of the neighbors. One wall of the living room was pink and the other side was yellow. The door was white on the inside and blue-green on the outside. When we brought this to her attention and told her that the colors did not go together, she answered, "It does not matter as long as it is clean." She did the same with the curtains that were given to her from the house that she cleaned. First they started by being too long for the window. Then, the second time she washed them, they were not only too short, but uneven. That, too, was all right as long as they were clean.

Everywhere we looked we saw the touch of my mother. Amá's hands even did the plumbing under the kitchen sink. We went a long time without the use of the sink. When we did use it we had to put a bucket underneath to catch the water. Amá would complain to the landlady and the response would be, "Don't worry, Elisa, soon I'll send somebody to fix it." That day never came.

This house did have indoor plumbing. The bathroom was very primitive, and we could see through the floor to the ground and watch the rats run by. The kitchen was crooked and lopsided, with drawers at such a tilt it was comical. These rooms were great for the cockroaches, as they could make a quick escape. The bedrooms were small, and order was necessary because there was no room for disorder. My mother slept with Estella in one room that was large enough for only one small bed. They had to sleep curled together like spoons in order to fit in the bed. I slept with Mary and Lisa in another bed. We slept with one leg on the next sister. We looked like figurines that became statues in the night, all facing the same direction. If one of us turned, we all had to turn. I was always stepping on someone's hair or leg. It was impossible to sleep without accidentally hitting someone, and we would wake up fighting with each other.

I still wonder why we had to learn so many lessons in this life. We left a neighborhood where abuse was the rule strictly followed, and moved only to find more daily pictures of people in the worst of situations. It was a place that spoke of debts bigger in size than the size of the rooms. Six apartments had six husbandless mothers, all with similar lives, all with children who never got to enjoy the innocence of childhood, only the struggle of living.

All of our teenage years were spent at this house on First Street with Amá, and then we learned to fly by ourselves, leaving Amá home. Sometimes we lied about our ages so we would get hired in the canneries. Those jobs were not any easier than fieldwork, but they were better paying. Some summers were better than others, but we always made sure Amá got our paychecks.

Across the border, the poverty of Mexico surrounded us. Barefoot children had been kept out of school, left to beg up and down the street for their daily needs. Their first classroom was the street. No flashcards, no books, no pencils or paper. Their life was raw survival. Homeless drunks crashed into garbage cans, and policemen kicked them in the backside or shoved them away since there was nothing of value to take from them.

My favorite scene was the game the immigration officials played with the Mexican workers. I called it hide-and-seek. It started as soon as the cover of darkness provided a mantle. While the government worked to patch the holes in the tall barrier that kept the workers from going back and forth, the workers were breaking a new hole through the wall all day a few miles away. At night, they would squeeze their plump, sweaty bodies through to the other side. The sound of a lunch box on metal marked the crossing of each one. Each thought himself lucky to beat the green immigration van and be on his way, swinging the lunch box and whistling a tune.

Other times the green van came silently, without lights, and the workers all scattered like cockroaches in the sudden flood of a spotlight. Often they made it across with their clothes in shreds from the ordeal. We could see them from our front window. Amá would rush out and offer the bushes of the backyard as a hiding place. She'd make it back to the house just in time to collect herself before the "seeker" patrols with their flashlights asked if she had witnessed the direction the "hiders" had taken. After they were gone, she would steer the fugitives in the opposite direction.

The noises from outside would wake us, along with the irritation to our noses from burning chorizo. Sometimes I would awaken to the smell of damp earth and find that Amá had watered the garden. This would tempt my appetite for a bit of *terrón de tierra* (a lump of clay). Sometimes we children would wake up and warn Amá that she was breaking the law by helping these fugitives. "Amá, you can get yourself in trouble with the law." Her answer was always "That's all right, my daughters, these people get hungry, too."

Monster Machines
~

Amá didn't know how to read, but she vividly remembered many tales her grandfather had told her. Grandfather told her that one day there would be machines that could fly like birds in the sky. Just like Abuelito told her about the airplanes, she told us about the "monster machines." Amá told us, "One day the monster machine will come and take away our jobs, so why worry about a few men who crawl through the fence?" We all thought she was making up stories to frighten us and make us work harder. She often told us scary tales so that we would listen to her. "If you do not obey me, I will ask your grandmother's soul to come pull on your toes while you sleep!"

She wasn't wrong about the monster machine. Soon we saw a huge cotton picker roll into the fields to replace the lifelong jobs of so many people. Sure enough, as she predicted, on a humid, predawn morning, Amá, my three sisters, and I arrived in the fields with our crumpled lunch bags in our hands, praying to be among those called to work. However, only a few other workers were chosen. Amá mourned that day as we walked back to the truck. We knew the struggles of our people against poverty would soon be multiplied.

As the trucks packed the workers back to town, Amá cried. My sister Mary tried to assure her that it wasn't the end. But even Mary knew that the ones not chosen faced a tomorrow that promised less than what they had yesterday. Still, she pointed out what a hard worker Amá was and how any foreman would be glad to have her working for him. Amá answered, "Yes, right now, but what will become of us who are getting older and can't read or write?"

To us girls, losing our jobs to the cotton machines meant not having money to buy material for new dresses. On the other hand, it also meant we were less likely to be caught with our working clothes plastered in mud from head to toe. We were always embarrassed to be seen by our friends from school because then they would know we worked in the fields. When we got off the truck and had to cross to the stores, we hid ourselves with scarves exposing only our eyes. We were only fooling ourselves, however, as the whole town knew we were field workers.

For Amá, losing our jobs meant watching us open an empty icebox, the landlord knocking at the door asking for the rent, no money for the bill that sat on the table saying "Final Notice" before the electricity would be shut off.

These events in Amá's life occurred during the 1960s. This was a time of enormous change in society and visionary leaders like John and Robert Kennedy. Amá didn't know much about politics, but the fact that the Kennedys were Catholics was good enough for her. Amá said that these men weren't just talking to hear themselves talk; they meant what they said. They promised to help the underprivileged. They gave hope to people like Amá, only to be struck down like martyred saints. There was also the turbulence of the Vietnam War. We didn't understand what the war was about. We only knew that some of our boys went to Vietnam and did not return alive.

One afternoon all of us girls were cooling off outside, eating watermelon and slapping the mosquitoes on our legs and foreheads. We heard a bunch of rockets, like when the carnival came to town, and saw kids running after a big white flatbed truck loaded with boxes. We followed along with the others to where it parked at the end of the street. Then a few men and women started handing out boxes of food containing cheese, powdered milk, rice, flour, beans, baby food, and peanut butter. The best part of all was that we could stand in line and no one asked questions. It felt like Christmas, and we ran home with our arms piled high. This program was started by President Kennedy to help the poor.

Then after his sudden death, it appeared as if the entire world stood still. It was so quiet that we could hear Amá striking the match as she lit her candle to honor him. Amá said he was too good to be on this earth. The same feelings and emotions came flooding back when Robert Kennedy was assassinated a few years later. From then on, Amá had us pray for them. She said their souls were like those of the saints who watch over us.

Meanwhile, we had our own hero, César Chávez, who stood up for people like us. He hurled us into the American mainstream by pushing the fight for human rights and our recognition as a people. The issues were poor wages and working conditions and the use of insecticides. Hundreds of workers organized themselves for change. The news media talked of violence, while strikers beat people with bats, turned over trucks, and torched the weeds along the riverbanks. They did this to frighten people, hoping to prevent them from crossing the picket lines. Friends were no longer friends if they crossed the picket lines, and workers were suspicious of each other and whispered among themselves.

Amá and her friend Doña Erlinda thought they could get away with one day's work before being found out. They arranged to go to work and got away with it for two days. They had to sneak around like fugitives in the dark, looking over their shoulders to make sure the strikers would not follow them and find out the location of their work truck. Sometimes the strikers did discover the trucks, and would set them on fire or hammer in the doors and break the windows. An even greater fear was of being ostracized by one's own people, making it then even harder to get a job.

Each day before Amá left, she had a list of precautions for us: "Don't forget to blow out the candle before you girls leave the house. Don't let the beans burn. Listen to your sister Mary when she tells you what to do." And she reminded us, "If anyone asks where I am, tell them I went to clean a house." Then we would plead with her, "Amá, don't go, you could get hurt!" She would always say, "I leave everything to God."

On the third day we discovered Amá by a palm tree. Her face was listless and defeated. Her brown eyes, usually so full of light, were now vacant and dull. She looked terribly hurt, as if she had been in a car wreck. She still held her smashed lunch bag in one hand, while the other held her ruined sombrero. She had been wearing it when her head was split open by a bat. Blood had streamed from her head and soaked her clothes. We ran to her, crying, "Amá, what happened?" "Daughters, it's nothing. It's just a bang on the head, just one hit." How like her to say it was nothing.

Once it became clear that the jobs weren't there anymore, people were forced to go north. For many people who crossed the border, not only their homes but also their families were lost. Children were sometimes left behind with grandparents, or husbands left their wives and children. They left to find jobs at restaurants, some of which should have been condemned for drainage problems and toilets that would overflow onto the floor. The men's feet would soak all day in this dirty water that reached up to their ankles. The Mexican who cleaned the floor was the same one who cleaned the dishes. The skin on the palms of his hands was already transparent, as if washing one more pan would tear the skin off altogether.

Jobs at the factory were a gamble too, for one never knew if he was going to make it to payday before the boss would turn him in to immigration to keep from having to pay his wages. The illegal immigrants tried to hide under the machines or inside boxes, but with no luck. Some might escape out the back door, while others just froze and were taken away to be sent back to Mexico without seeing a penny for all their work. The boss would drain the life from their bodies, giving them the worst positions. These workers handled whatever toxic product needed to be handled or spread. The chemicals would eat at their hands, and they would acquire lumps all over their bodies.

Hunger made them fear losing their jobs. The worst conditions in the United States were better than what they had left behind. Many families were able to save what they earned and were able to build homes. But some women never heard from their husbands again. These men would set up new homes and families, forgetting about the worn-out women they had left behind to fend for themselves and their children. Other men were simply too ashamed to return home empty-handed. Unfortunately, this desperation for progress is the same today as it was forty years ago.

Meanwhile, the children who were left behind withdrew from school. The girls became somebody's servant, perhaps the boss's little playmate. The girls who did not find work as servants often sold themselves at the cantinas at the age of thirteen or fourteen. The boys learned to steal and cheat to help their mothers with the other children. The tragedy of this country was that this poverty cheapened all the values of life. I now understand what Amá meant when she said how lucky we were to be born on the U.S. side of the fence. It was our destiny.

Amá paid very little attention to her own needs, but there were two things she never denied herself. She listened to the music of northern Mexico at four A.M. each morning, and she tended her plants. And there were the many moments when, side-by-side, we were preparing the chiles for her secret recipes and she would wrap herself in the memories of her lost childhood. When the chiles boiled over, she would snap back to reality as the dancing and crackling of the burned chiles pierced her daydreams.

My whole object in life was to make a fast escape and be with my friends. Still, sometimes she would stop me and make me promise that when she came to her last place of rest, a band of mariachis would lead her to heaven. *"Promételo."* ("Promise me this.") I would promise just to get away. Or sometimes I would ask, "Why do you talk this way?" She only replied, *"Promételo."* If I had listened a little more closely, I would have sensed how homesick she was in spirit. The music she listened to was all about her *tierra* and her *ranchito*.

But this was not the time of my life to sense the longings of my mother. It was a time that I was centered on myself and making sure that my friends' boobs hadn't grown bigger than mine in the last twenty-four hours.

Menstrual Wars

~

With time, my sisters and I changed from *niñas* to *mujeres* with the start of our menstrual period, what Amá called *"la maldición"* ("the curse"). This affliction came upon us without warning and caused a war that lasted for years. Amá had her hands full, with five fierce and angry women who were at all times ready to pull each other's hearts out at the slightest provocation. It only took one wrong word, one touch or look, to ignite our years of unresolved anger. We communicated physically and destructively. Handy household items fell victim to our moods, one after another.

Each year we bought a new ornament for the Christmas tree, but one particular Christmas we decided to share our money and make ornaments for the tree. Amá was working, so Estella, Mary, and I spent many hours making popcorn and cherry garlands for the tree. When we finished decorating the little pine, we couldn't agree on the proper corner for it. My sister Estella was beside herself because she couldn't get the Christmas tree to stand straight in the bucket. After so many tries and one last nasty word from me, she became so angry she grabbed the tree and began swinging it at us as if it were a baseball bat and we were elusive balls. We screamed and jumped from bed to bed as she chased us. She finally flung the humble tree out the door. We stopped running, stunned at the sight of the poor little tree with the shattered ornaments and crushed popcorn and cherry strings on its side beneath a swaying palm.

While the Christmas tree incident was explained away to the neighbors, the slingshot incident was something else. This was another example of runaway emotions that came with the monthly "visitor." One hot summer Saturday, my mother and her gossiping friends stood outside fanning themselves and moving along with the shade of the palm tree while they complained, "When will we get out of this hell?"

I was sitting by the open window when I saw Stella in the backyard, poised with a slingshot, aiming at a nest of baby birds. She took a shot, knocking them to the ground. I ran yelling outside and saw that the parched ground was scattered with little dead birds. Stella shoved me aside as I grabbed for the weapon, all the time hollering for her to stop. She cursed back, telling me, "Shut up! If you don't, I'm going to shoot you!" I turned and ran for Amá, but Stella was quicker. Before I could get to Amá, a Seven-Up bottle meant for me whizzed past my ear and narrowly missed her friend's forehead.

To the woman it was as if the devil himself had thrown it. Her words burned like fire as she spewed out the malediction, "Your hand will wither and die for what you have done!" In her anger, she tripped over a chair, her eyes blazing and her mouth screaming in indignation as though the world was coming to an end. "This generation has lost all respect for their elders!" As she yelled "*¡muchacho!*" and "*¡grosera!*" my sister replied defiantly, "I have the devil in me but you have a big mouth!" Poor Amá could only look on in horror and shame.

Then there was Mary. Mary and I had one thing in common—we both owned certain possessions that we did not want anyone to touch. Mary's treasures were her two strapless bras, which she wore only on weekends with her spaghetti strap dresses. She won lots of attention from the boys, and all of us younger girls were in awe. The only things she seemed to have that we didn't were developed breasts. So whenever we got the chance, we would sneak her bras to our friends' houses and stuff them full of tissue. As careful as we might be, she'd discover them missing and would search until she found us. She wasn't subtle about it—she'd just collar us, grab the tissue out, and unsnap the bra. After she had her bra back, she'd drag us home by the hair while we cried and begged for mercy.

I kept my precious possessions in a cigar box in a particular dresser drawer. My marauding sisters may have been looking for money, but all they would find were the memorabilia that captured the essence of my young heartthrob. From junior high through high school I loved a certain neighbor boy from afar. I collected candy wrappers he had touched, pencils he had left behind, his study notes—anything of his I could get my hands on. He grew into a stunning athlete who was sometimes featured in the newspaper. Clippings of these articles and photos were my greatest treasures. He never knew of my passion for him, though we were friends and saw each other constantly.

When I detected the slightest sign that someone had gone through my drawer, I'd feel the blood rush to my head and that familiar anger rising to the surface. The room would rattle with my screams as I demanded to know who the culprit was. Amá tried to keep peace, saying, "*Hija*, that is not important. Everything is like you left it." This would only make my temper hotter. "So what are you going to do about it?" Stella asked. I just threw myself at her like a lion, hitting her with anything handy. She didn't seem to understand that these were the only things I had that were totally mine. Amá would cry, "Daughters, please! You're going to kill me by making me so angry!"

Thinking back, I don't know how Amá survived all of this. Everything to us seemed like the end of the world. We put her through hell with our expressions of anger. There were times when we would resort to fistfighting, and my Amá would get in the middle and end up thrown on the bed like an old doll.

Since respecting my drawer was not important to Stella, I adopted the same attitude toward her one pair of shiny loafers. These penny loafers were supposed to be untouchable, but every now and then I would sneak them out and wear them downtown. They were too small but I'd squeeze my feet into them. One Sunday afternoon I was feeling very cool, looking down every couple of minutes at the beautiful shoes as my friend and I walked to the movie theater. Suddenly, Stella was there, teetering toward me in her first pair of white high heels, her bouffant hairdo bobbing as she walked. She loudly demanded that I take off her shoes. I protested, "No, I can't wear high heels!" But she said, "Fine, then walk home barefoot," and she grabbed the shoes from me. So there I was—a thirteen-year-old with a halter top, a bowl haircut, stick legs, and no choice but to wobble home in 110° F heat. When I got there, the real fight began. We screamed at each other, until finally I threw Amá's cook pot at Stella, hitting her on the shoulder. She grabbed scissors and threw them at me, striking my elbow but luckily not cutting me.

Life is amazing! My sisters and I not only survived those stormy years, but now we laugh when we look back at our experiences. We realize that as hard as our lives were, we grew stronger and closer to each other because of it.

~

AS TEARS BURN in my eyes now, I think, "Oh, Amá, it was so easy for me to blame you for everything that went wrong in my life. As a child I couldn't get close to you because you seemed to be always leaving, always out of my reach. I was so angry with you for putting other people before us. You would believe them when they accused us of things we didn't do. When you whipped me, an innocent, for stealing the neighbor's carnival tickets, I started building a wall between us. When you showed no remorse for the injustice, how could I trust you again? And the more my father bruised your heart, the angrier you became. I could not help that I was a constant reminder of my father to you. You never failed to tell me this when you were angry with me. '*Eres como tu padre—mal!*' ('You're like your father—bad!')"

One of the most significant events in a young Catholic girl's life was the celebration of the Virgin Mary's birthday. I dreamed of the time when I would be old enough to participate in the procession of girls who brought her flowers. I wondered, Would I ever be one of the twelve who were chosen? Everyone would stop and focus on the girls as they entered the church with their long pastel-colored chiffon gowns flowing behind them as they moved down the aisle. They proceeded into the church to the chiming of bells and heavenly strains of music to the statue of our Lady, feeling as though they were entering into heaven itself. Candles flickered and incense burned, mingling with the glorious scents of flowers brought from every home in town. These girls resembled pure, radiant angels waiting to see their Mother Mary appear, each one offering her own bouquet of flowers, held so delicately in her hands.

When I was fourteen years old, May finally arrived and I was picked to walk in the procession. I remembered racing home to tell Amá that I had been picked. I looked for her in the kitchen where she always was, but she fooled me. So I ran out, slamming the screen door, and heard her shout, "Can't you see the door is already loose?" I looked toward the garage and there was Amá, in her light blue housedress with her hair halfway rolled in a twist. She was in the garage soaking the white clothes in bleach. She didn't even turn to hear what I had to say to her. Instead, she continued to work at the rusty, worn washboard, oblivious to my words and my excitement. When I told her the requirement for being in the procession was a brand-new dress and shoes, she said in an exasperated tone, "Oh, this is too much for us. We can't afford a new dress. Borrow one from one of your friends."

All the years of looking forward to this honor faded at that moment. I was instantly furious. My tongue ran faster than my mind, and the words just poured out. All of those times of "no, we can't" came boiling to the surface. I screamed that it was her fault that we didn't have more in this life and her fault that we didn't have a father. I knew it wasn't true. Amá slapped me across the face and still I screamed. I pushed her out of the way. I left the yard, feeling the intense May heat outside that matched my own temperature inside.

I sat on the curb at the water hydrant and watched a stream of water run over my feet and down the street on this suffocating early summer evening. My mind felt empty, yet heavy, as if it had turned into cement. I began pulling my hair. I didn't know if it was she I hated or myself. I was full of resentment and confusion. I wanted a dress. I wanted her to be able to pay the bills, but there was no money for both. I behaved like a barefoot beast, dressed in a T-shirt and shorts. I pulled my hair and felt the water pressure on my feet as the anger seethed inside. I pulled my hair harder, this time with both hands. I scratched and bit myself. I wanted to purge the poison from my system. I asked the water, the earth, and the trees, "When will this miserable life be over? Is this the only way of life for us?"

Amá surrendered to my fury. She gave me the gas and electricity money to have a dress made. After all of those years of anticipation, I walked in my new dress with an empty feeling. I felt I had stolen something from my *amá*. That event that I had thought was so crucial to my happiness left me in a far worse place, a place of debt. Not knowing how to mend the situation, I acted the only way I knew how. In my pride I resented my sense of indebtedness to her, and I became more hateful as each day passed. It was here that I completed building the wall that separated us. I knew I could never look into her eyes again.

Now I realize that I was too ashamed and embarrassed to say I was sorry. It was easier for me to stay angry. The years passed, and our long distance conversations over the telephone were shorter and shorter, so full of emptiness.

While the other women in my family managed to let go of the hurts of their past, I seem to have carried with me a burden of resentment and anger for all of us. They took comfort in forgetting and focusing on what life had to offer, leaving behind dark caves full of pain. But I have been driven to fight the dragons that lurk within. My sense of justice will not allow me to run from them. I have learned to use my anger as a weapon to battle the demons of my past, to fight for my self-worth—and by facing them, to ultimately walk out of their shadows.

Graduations
~

Mary's last year of school came, with the chance to finally be liberated from all of us. All that Amá demanded of us was that we get through high school. After that, there were two things that society predetermined for a girl: she either got married, had children, and dreamed of what life could have been, or, if she was fortunate, she might get one of the few jobs available. One such job was working in the utility office, sharing a room with the same person day after day. The most prestigious job was working for the Immigration and Naturalization Service, where one would deal with thousands of people, eventually seeing them turn from human beings into green cards. Only a handful of jobs were available, and those who were hired would lift their arms and bless the skies for their luck. They would stay in those jobs until their bodies became stiff and their hands crippled.

Mary's career came from heaven. Amá had said that if you loved your job and were good at what you did, it was a special gift from God. Mary put herself through beauty school. She attended classes during the day and worked in the evening, helping Amá to feed and clothe us. The year slipped by quickly, and Mary completed her course and was ready to go into practice. Her gift was to create art from hair. Her hands would make people look and feel beautiful. She could bring out the best from the least.

Mary entertained us daily with stories about her old biddies. They became a part of our lives. We knew about Mrs. Rogers, who had three hairs on her head but wanted hair like Elizabeth Taylor's. There was Wilma, who complained that the economy was eating her up. She thought Mary owed her a miracle for her twenty-five-cent tip, painfully given, her turkey-foot hand shaking with the effort of parting with the coin. Mary did not know what to do with those bags of saggy skin. In those days, wrinkles could not be folded or tucked away. Then there was Miss Dorothy, who wanted her hair to look like her white poodle's. She insisted that Mary use the fanciful pink or blue color rinses to match the bows on her dog's ears, and she wanted her hair fluffed like her dog's. Mary tried to tell her that it wasn't in her best interest, because her hair was thin and if she teased it any higher, she would end up looking like a scared, hairless greyhound.

Mary ultimately had to return to God his gift, when she

grew tired of the patrons blaming her hairstyles for their old looks. Late one Saturday we saw her come home with her black hairdressing kit in her hand. She walked into the house, collapsed in a chair, and said, "No more! No more old biddies for me!" She took off her white shoes and uniform and threw them in the trashcan. "They are lucky that I am quitting before I yank out the three hairs they have left on their heads!" She went to work full-time at the five-and-ten-cent store.

Mary stayed home for a few more years, helping to see all of us through high school. I can't say when things changed, but gradually my mother became the daughter and Mary became the mother. Mary, who had poured out her soul for her family, found a man who gave his to her. He lived by the same principles that she did, and they respected each other. Life rewarded Mary with a soul mate. His name is Manuel.

Manuel had a natural beauty radiating from his golden brown eyes, eyes that many years later still had a youthful quality. He was tall and slim, his hands long and masculine, yet very gentle. His voice was quiet and low, and his sparse words were well chosen. He made Amá's life more comfortable, giving so much of himself. He was so sensitive to Amá's feelings he could know what she wanted without her speaking. He gave up vacations to take care of her, spending many sleepless nights with her while she was ill. To her, he was an angel walking on this earth. To the rest of us, he was our second brother. From these two, Mary and Manuel, came two sons who learned to honor Amá. Just as their grandmother had demanded that we finish high school, she expected the sons of Mary and Manuel to finish college, and they did.

The year Estella graduated from high school we all went up to Hollister to work in the canneries. When the season was over, she was determined to follow her dream to become an airline stewardess. She refused to be discouraged by the librarian who scoffed at her daydreams some years before. She informed us that she was moving to Los Angeles. We all laughed at her because she had no money and knew no one there, but two days later she was on her way.

Estella would hear none of our forebodings and fears—that she'd get lost or that she'd fall in with weird people. We were genuinely worried that we'd never see her again, but she simply let our words run in one ear and out the other. She put on her leather boots, tucked her hip-hugger jeans inside those boots, packed her two bags, grabbed her sunglasses, and slid her bag onto her shoulder. We saw her walk away looking like such a free spirit that it made me realize that I could do the same thing someday.

Amá stayed out on the corner of the street until she saw the last of Estella's long black hair disappear into the distance on the road to the bus depot. She came back blessing Estella, asking God to take care of all of us because we were growing up and she could no longer tell us what to do.

Stella landed in East Los Angeles, on Ford Whittier Avenue, and ended up living in an apartment that had a mixture of residents, from junkies and prostitutes to religious cultists and fanatics. She found a job in a movie theater, working her way up from ticket seller to manager. Stella would always call with excitement, telling us how well she was doing.

~

IN 1967 I was marking time as I waited to graduate so I could start my exciting life, too. I didn't know where I was going to get the money or what I was going to do after graduation, but I knew I'd be leaving home. My best friends, Jennie and Sylvia, were planning to go to the Montebello Dental Assistant School in Los Angeles, and I decided to enroll, too. My brother came up with my tuition for the course. Our heads were filled with the optimism of youth, but we had no money in our pockets for traveling and living expenses.

Suddenly, the opportunity presented itself at the wedding

reception of another girlfriend of ours, Nena. There, we learned that the newlyweds were heading out on their honeymoon, going in the same direction we wanted to go, so we approached the honeymooners with the idea of hitching a ride with them. They tried to give us all the excuses in the world why they couldn't give us a ride, but we badgered them until finally they gave in. We quickly packed, and we were ready when they said to be ready. We were not going to lose this great chance.

Everything started out fine as the five of us, our worldly belongings stuffed in sacks, crammed ourselves into the newlyweds' car, with tin cans and pom-poms and crepe paper hanging off the back. Not long down the road, however, the couple didn't seem to be as happy as they were at the reception. The silence of the newlyweds sitting solemnly in the front seat was deafening. We three clueless girls in the back seat interpreted their silence as fatigue and continued to chatter away like magpies.

About two hours into our four-hour trip, the 1961 Chevy drove into a filling station just outside Palm Springs. In 1967, Palm Springs was not the metropolis it later became. It was a small town in the middle of the desert. Nena and her husband got out of the car and seemed to be having an intense conversation while the car was being filled with gas. Then they got back in the car and we set off down the road.

Not too much farther from the filling station, Nena's husband stopped the car. Then he turned around in his seat and very deliberately told us that we needed to get out because that was as far as they were going with us. We tried to object, but our words came out in a series of "uhs" as we were deposited in the desert at three in the morning, with miles of bare road on either side. The stars twinkled, and we could hear the sounds of the desert as wildlife came alive in the cool morning air.

We no sooner had our bags out of the car than Nena and

her new husband peeled out and left us in the dust. We were dumbfounded by the speed of their decision and exit. We realized we were in the middle of nowhere. We started walking and complaining, walking and complaining. We put our thumbs out to signal the rare car that drove by. An hour passed, and we still didn't have a ride. The situation seemed hopeless. Then, along came a big gray Cadillac that passed us, but then stopped and reversed direction. The driver looked like an elderly Kenny Rogers, with white hair and a pompadour. He wore a heavy gold watch and cowboy boots. He asked us where we were going, and we told him Los Angeles. To our relief, he told us to get in the car. We were so impressed with the plush burgundy seat covers.

Fortunately this man was a gentleman who gave us a fatherly lecture about not riding with strangers. He took us directly to Stella's apartment in East Los Angeles. The neighborhood where Stella lived did not match her descriptions on the phone. To say she lived on the wrong side of the tracks was a big understatement. The desert looked good compared to this area.

We entered the building where Stella rented an old, tired efficiency apartment. We had to climb over passed-out druggies and up a stairway ripe with the smells of booze, cigarettes, and old, stale garbage to get to the manager's apartment. We knocked on the door and a huge, fat man answered. He looked like he was high on heroin. He led us to Stella's room and opened the door. Stella wasn't there. We scavenged for food but the cupboards were bare. We put together enough change to hit the doughnut shop and buy cheap day-old doughnuts. Stella didn't return until midnight. She was surprised and embarrassed that we saw firsthand where she was living. It didn't match up to the rosy descriptions she gave in her letters.

The next day, we took the bus to the Montebello Dental Assistant School to begin classes. Our trio learned to take X-rays and take molds for dentures, and learned the names and uses of all kinds of dental tools. We studied and studied, and all three of us did well. Meanwhile, though, we took part-time jobs. I worked at a wig store styling wigs. Sylvia got a job at a clothing store, and Jenny got a job filing insurance claims. All three of us continued to live with Stella, and our waist-lines thickened with cheap doughnuts that, along with oat-meal and water, became the staples of our diet.

When I graduated, I was placed as an intern with an old troll of a dentist in an old dilapidated building in downtown Los Angeles. When I walked in the office in my clean, white uniform and brand-new nurse's shoes, I knew I was in trouble. There was no receptionist, no tidy waiting room, and no pictures on the walls. I timidly called, "Hello, hello!" Eventually my miniature "boss" emerged from the back and barked at me to get to work. He expected me to answer the phone and know my way around the office, as though I had worked there for years.

In school we worked on dummies and each other. My first patient in the real world of dentistry was a very large man with three chins. He plopped down in an old, broken-down dental chair that I could barely pump two inches off the floor due to his massive size. When I took X-rays of his teeth, I told him to bite down on the film, but he chomped down on my finger like a pit bull before I could pull it out of his mouth. The absurdity of the situation made both my first patient and me get the giggles. Nothing at the Montebello Dental Assistant School prepared me for a near finger amputation. The dentist burst into the room, annoyed with the racket we were making. He didn't appreciate the humor.

My next task was to assist this diminutive dentist with a tooth extraction. As I was handing him the instruments, I couldn't concentrate on anything but the blood dripping out of the patient's mouth. After that ordeal was over I went to wash the instruments in a little, dark room with a tiny, rusty sink. When I was finished and was starting to dry them, my boss came running into the room shouting, "Money! Money!" I looked around, thinking that money was miraculously appearing somewhere, but he was pointing to the dripping faucet. "You're throwing money down the drain!"

I worked in that crazy place until lunchtime. Then I walked out the door, went home, and never came back. In fact, I threw my new nurse's shoes and uniform in the trash and put my career as a dental assistant permanently out to lunch.

My part-time job at Stacy and Stewart's Wig Shop became full-time. I styled movie stars' wigs and was promoted to manager of the shop. I had a hot pink uniform and a wild beehive hairstyle with cascading curls and bows. I was hot and successful! Stacy and Stewart even gave me a key to the store.

Meanwhile, Jenny and Sylvia discovered they hated being dental assistants, too. They quit their dental assistant jobs and turned their part-time, temporary jobs at the insurance company and the clothing store into full-time work.

The Curse
~

By this time my father had disappeared completely from our lives. We heard through family members that he had become a recluse in the Valle de Guadalupe, along with the even more incredible story that he had become a minister and lived off the land now. He had dragged along his last party girl, who became his live-in maid. It had to stay that way, because he still considered himself married to Amá even though they had been separated for fifteen years. Amá referred to him as *"ese hombre"* ("that man").

Apá had moved, we were told, to a dreadful hole of a place, a piece of hidden desert. The land was powdery, bare of growing things, without houses or paths. All day he fought the dust in his mouth and eyes. There was no way to combat the blazing sun. There was no shelter from it in his roofless brick house. In the heat of the burning sun, Apá worked along in his fields. At fifty-eight, he labored, with his eyes nailed to the ground, in salty clothes stained with sweat. His hard, dry hands were indistinguishable from the ground itself. He tilled the parched and hostile fields with a pick and shovel.

He must have hoped that distance could undo a lifetime of cruelties, abuse, abandonment, utter lack of conscience. But no pounding of his heart or walking on his knees could erase the memories of the torture he inflicted on others. The reality was that he was a man who hated women. Perhaps his quest was to get even with all women for what his mother had done to him. He relived the pain he, a bastard child, had gone through until his heart was hollow and shrunken. He passed on his ache by bringing into the world twenty-one living children and supporting none of us. He kept his hate going by substituting vengeance for conscience. I am one of his five surviving legitimate children, thanks to Amá.

In the end, nothing helped him to escape *la maldición*, the curse of self-destruction that he had brought upon himself. Ultimately, Apá died alone. He was fried and tossed to the ground while working on a power pole.

About his demise Amá said, "As you live, so shall you die."

My Knight in Shining Armor

~

One fateful Easter Sunday, I was babysitting the autistic son of the apartment manager and gazing out the window at people coming and going in their Sunday best, when I spotted a tall, muscular man with silky, long black hair, brown bell-bottoms, and a velour shirt. I thought for sure he was a Hollywood star without a contract, slumming in my own neighborhood. He was standing in his Converse tennis shoes by the stinky garbage, waiting for a ride. I took a double-take at this man and declared to myself, "He will be the father of my children." This handsome stranger left, and I returned to the business of taking care of the little boy who rocked back and forth and never looked me in the eye.

I could not wait to share with my friend Jenny that I had seen my Mexican in shining armor. He would be the man to deliver me from East L.A. When Jenny got home, I described this man of my dreams. To my surprise, Jenny knew him and told me, "Oh, that's José."

I asked her, "How do you know him, Jenny?"

"Oh, he lives downstairs in apartment number one."

I could hardly wait for her to introduce us. I begged Jenny to arrange a way for us to meet. She just wanted to introduce me directly, but I wanted it to look like a chance meeting.

In those days, you could get money from deposits on soda bottles. We would collect not only our own but others we found in alleys or garbage cans. When we had enough of them, we'd take them back to the doughnut shop or another store to get the refunds. It was a way to get bus fare for the week. We had a number of these bottles that had to be returned, and we used this as an excuse to pass this handsome fellow in the alley. I remember that as I got nearer to him, I was mesmerized by his face. He had the sweetest smile. Jenny and he greeted each other before she introduced me.

Jenny invited José to the apartment to watch TV at about seven P.M. He knocked on the door, and the moment I saw him, I felt numb and stupid and giddy. Desire had taken over my senses. José was a grand talker and talked for hours, telling us what he did for his work and why he was in L.A. for the summer. We learned he had come to the United States that semester to work and take some English courses. He found a job laying carpet for a company, and he lived with seven other men in an apartment downstairs.

José saw the United States as a land of opportunity. However, he didn't like the fact that here, people didn't take the time to live; it was all about work. He favored Mexico for the slower pace and the way people took time to live life. He enjoyed the freedom from rules in Mexico—at least there was nothing that couldn't be settled if you had money in your wallet.

José sounded so intelligent to me. He talked about his classmates and how they were all going to become dentists, doctors, and lawyers. Right away that impressed me. He told me about the state he came from, Michoacán. He said his father was very wealthy.

I couldn't believe my good fortune. I thought, "Oh my God, this man is handsome, intelligent, and rich!" And that smile that he had . . . When he smiled with his eyes closed, I was taken in, way beyond the point of no return.

That day we became a pair, and, thereafter, this poor guy was using his extra money to take my two girlfriends and me to dinner every other night. He would take us to have big, fat, juicy beef *tacos de machaca.* After the third dinner, he asked if he could speak to me privately. He then announced, "You know what, I am dating you, I am not dating your two friends, too, so I'm not taking them to dinner anymore." That day I broke my promise to Jenny and Sylvia to let them tag along on dates so that they could get a free meal. They, too, were penniless but the free meals had to end.

José and I dated for the next three months, and the more I listened to him and his stories, the deeper in love I fell. He was well read, and he was my own Socrates. He questioned the world and told me about Greek philosophers. He read poetry to me. He talked about World War II and the Mexican-American War as if he had fought in both. He was a student of all the U.S. presidents.

At the end of three months, his summer work was over, and it was time for José to return to Mexico to finish his college studies. I decided I'd see him off as far as the U.S.-Mexican border. I was wearing a white, flowered minidress and some flip-flops. We got as far as Calexico on the Greyhound bus, and I couldn't bear to let his hand go. There at the bus station, he arose to leave. I could feel my heart breaking in pieces. He must have felt the same way, or so I thought, because he asked, "Would you like to come with me?" It didn't take me even a second to say yes, and my feet were on the stairs of the bus.

When the bus pulled away, my conscience started talking to me. It was the middle of the night, and there was no going back. I was sure that Mother Mary was looking at me, and my brother Joe was chasing after the bus to catch me. We traveled and traveled. We arrived in José's state in the middle of the night.

I had heard Mexico was beautiful, and he had told me that where he came from was very beautiful, but it didn't take me long to appreciate that beauty is in the eyes of the beholder. When we got to José's little town in Michoacán, we found that the town had no electricity. The power had gone out, and the entire town was dark—no lights. And it was ominously thundering like there was a war in heaven. I should have known then it was bad luck.

It felt to me like a dungeon where Dracula lived. The streets were narrow, rocky, and unpaved. The buildings looked like prisons, with little windows side-by-side, the size of bricks, made out of glass. The doors were made out of heavy iron and were almost as tall as the buildings. We walked through many little streets until we got to his corner, with a little street sign that said, "Calle de Insurgentes."

We arrived at his house, where we knocked and knocked until his father, Adolfo, finally appeared. He was an older man with gray hair and a very refined facial bone structure. He had a soft, quiet voice and a stern demeanor, like a war colonel. After he gave José a stiff and short embrace, he turned around and looked at me in a puzzled way, rudely asking of his son, "And what is this?"

José said, "Oh, I bring with me *mi novia.*" The old gentleman didn't even bother to look at my face or give me a nice greeting. We walked inside the house, into rooms of cement walls with tiny little glass block windows, and I thought to myself, "What in the world have I done? If José thinks they're rich, how do the poor live?"

If I thought I had come from a dysfunctional family, spending a few weeks there taught me to love my America and my home. It took me one day to see the obvious—women did not have a voice there, and only the man of the house received respect. Mr. Adolfo was everything and the others were nothing. The two sisters-in-law who lived there with their families had conformed themselves to Adolfo's moods. They hated yet respected him at the same time. He was served his food first and ate the best of what they had. The best piece of meat was saved for him. The cream off the milk was given to him. Every day he came home drunk and would pick a fight in the streets. Sometimes he would be in a crazy state and accuse his wife of having two sons that were not his. Even though these boys looked exactly like him, he seemed to need some excuse for beating his wife. He was like a cruel dictator.

There was so much tension in that house. The occupants

were like little rats, cowering in their hole until the cat left so they could come out and play. While he was home, they abided by his demands: Don't talk around him, don't turn the music on, and don't watch television. He bathed first, ate first, and selected the TV programs.

His wife tiptoed around him as if she was walking on eggshells. She covered her bowed head with a dark rebozo and wore a long dress. Just to hear this tyrant's voice would make her nervous, and she would forget what she was doing. She was so consumed with fear that she had no loyalty or attachment to her six kids—they raised themselves out in the streets. The lady was never allowed to go see her own family, who lived nearby. She would send little messages with a servant to see how her father was doing. She was allowed to go to church only for the mass held at five o'clock in the morning. If her husband caught her even stepping out of her door to talk to her neighbors, he'd deliver a beating. He kept her in fear and isolation from the neighbors.

From my perspective, life got worse day by day. But as for these women, they had accepted this life as normal. They were in a relative comfort zone and walked through their life like robots. There I was with my minidress, makeup, and teased hair. To them, I was nothing but a low-class prostitute. It didn't take me long to know I wasn't wanted. Adolfo advised his son not to marry this whore from the United States. Moreover, the sisters-in-law who lived under Adolfo's roof were not allowed to talk to me. I was like a disease to all of them and had no one to offer me friendship, not even José. Adolfo paid him to leave me.

My knight in shining armor turned into the devil in those six weeks, and my grand ideas of the life I had hoped for quickly dissipated. I certainly had second thoughts about José being the father of my children, but it was too late. A baby was on the way.

I called my mother, and my family arranged to get me a ticket home. My mother met me in Guadalajara. Her acceptance of my condition wasn't easy because in those times pregnancy out of wedlock invited gossip, shame, and embarrassment. It took a while for my mother to forgive me.

I can remember that bus ride back to Calexico. I felt like my heart and spirit had flown out of me. I was numb and disappointed by the great deception life had played on me. I kept saying to myself, "I deserve this; I deserve this. I should have listened to my friends and family instead of my heart and José's tall tales."

As things settled down between Amá and me, and with the baby growing inside of me, I began to see hope in life again. Eight months later, during the month of St. Joseph, I was blessed with a baby boy whom I named José. When I heard my baby cry I felt that I had found love for the first time.

The Reunion
~

One summer evening when Little José was seven months old, I ran across the border to Mexicali to buy some groceries. When I returned, Amá told me about several phone calls in which she could hear someone breathing. She'd ask, "*¿Quién habla? ¿Quién habla?*" No one answered her and she'd hang up the telephone.

Not long after she told me this, the phone again rang. This time, I picked up the receiver. I could hear somebody breathing; a weird feeling came over me and I asked, "Is this you, José?"

He answered quietly, "*Sí, soy yo.*"

I asked him, "Where are you calling from?"

He said, "From across the fence in front of your house." He asked me if I could come and see him in the park.

I told him, "Sure."

As I hung up the phone, my body erupted in emotion. Thoughts and feelings spewed out of me like hot lava, and rumblings of fear and anger surfaced in a way that I hardly expected. I shook with anger. I shuddered in fear. I had rehearsed to myself over and over what I would say if I ever saw him again. I'd tell him, "You coward! You weren't man enough to stand by me when I was pregnant. You weren't big enough to deliver the news that you never intended to marry me. Instead, you had that swine you call your father do it. You, who bragged about your money, left me without a penny in that cage you call home. I had to ask my mother to send me money to get out of there. I had to face my brother, who had warned me you were no good. I endured the shame of being a mother all alone. You cannot imagine how alone I felt." I trembled all over as I prepared to see this squirrel on whom I had focused my anger, fear, and shame these many months.

José did not look like I remembered him. He was thinner. His hair was now short and unkempt. His beige shirt did not complement his yellow-brown skin. His polyester brown pants were nothing like the tight bell-bottoms he used to wear. His once bright eyes were not as enchanting as I remembered them. They seemed dull and lifeless. I was so prepared to give him a piece of my mind, but, at the sight of him, instead, I felt only pity. He seemed weak and pathetic, a shadow of what he had been.

I confronted him, "Why did you come?"

He replied meekly, "I'm sorry I left you and my son. I imagine him every time I see children at play. I can't have fun with my friends while thinking of both of you. School isn't even going well for me."

He hung his head and tears streamed down his cheeks. He begged, "Give me another chance; give me another chance. I'll do anything you want me to. I'll be the father to my son that my father wasn't to me. I want to be there for his first day at school. I want to see him grow. When he graduates from high school, I want him to see my face. I want him to feel smart and proud. Please, give me another chance."

I kept telling him "no," but he wore me down with his apologies and promises to change. Finally, I said, "I'll think about this but I need to talk with my family."

He told me he'd return in three days for my answer. During this time, my uncles, brother, and mother tried to discourage me from returning to Big José. They said, "*Niña*, you are both Mexicans, but you come from two different worlds. Here, you are used to freedom. Where he grew up, women were seen but not heard." They reminded me how he ran away from responsibility once and that he'd do it again. But my overriding wish was for Little José to have a father. I knew that and my family knew that.

Big José saw this as a vulnerability he could exploit. He promised this time he'd be there for us. We'd move to Chicago, where his older brother, Roberto, held work as a pressman for a printing company. "He has promised me he'll get me a job with him," José told me. I agreed to leave my family home in Calexico on the condition that he would not take me back to Mexico. I momentarily forgot how his father treated his mother and other women. I was too young to understand that to José wife-abuse was normal, infidelity acceptable, and anger the only male emotion allowed.

We left for Chicago without Amá's blessing. Sure enough, the job Roberto promised was waiting for José in the Windy City.

Marriage and Children

~

Big José wanted a second child, but I hesitated. He had abandoned me once when I was pregnant, and I feared he'd do it again. We were also too poor to afford a second child, let alone send both children to college.

However, on one of José's more charismatic days, he wooed me with the promise of a diamond ring. I asked, "How big?"

He replied, "Don't worry. It will be a good size." With that, I got my most precious stone, my daughter, Debbie. The actual diamond never came.

In Chicago, our relationship was simply surviving, without passion or any real emotional attachment. One day, to my surprise, José arrived home with a big box. I was so excited to get this gift. It was like Christmas in June.

However, when I opened the box, my jaw dropped and my eyes widened. Inside the box was the ugliest brown polyester shirtwaist dress I ever saw. The top had cream, orange, and yellow flowers, and the skirt was solid chocolate brown with a big patent leather waist belt similar to Santa Claus's. He bought me brown-and-cream suede boots to match. He said, "Here, put this on. Put this on."

I tried on this ridiculous outfit. I felt like Carmen Miranda, missing only the bananas on top of my head. I blurted out, "I'm not wearing this. The colors are all wrong for me. All you'll be able to see are my white teeth." He didn't hear one thing I said.

I was still wondering why he bought this getup, but he cleared that up right away. "Our wedding is in one hour down at the courthouse!" he pronounced. I was rather dazed and confused. It all seemed so abrupt. My wedding was more of an order than a request. It was as if I had no say in this day that every little girl dreams about. I had no white dress, no veil, no wedding cake, and no say in my future. Everything had been arranged, down to this ridiculous outfit so far removed from my taste. I had longed to give my children a legal father but this wedding seemed so sudden.

We took the elevated train from Ashland to the courthouse in downtown Chicago for the ceremony. I was so glad I didn't know anybody who would recognize me in that crazy getup. In our haste, we forgot that we needed wedding bands. We used a pearl ring and my graduation ring as symbols of our undying love. After the fifteen-minute ceremony, José kissed me on the cheek. The judge urged us to "do better" but we were both too shy to kiss in front of this important man. These were some of the best memories I ever had in my life with José.

We left the courthouse with ten dollars in our pockets. José gave me a choice for postnuptial activities. We could take the El home or go out for a hot dog and soda and walk home. I chose the hot dog, and we laughed and giggled as we ate our wedding dinner, mustard dripping from our fingers.

José and I spent the next four years in Chicago. He continued to work at the printing company, and I got a job at a day-care center. There I learned that rich people have problems too. Parents with brand-new cars and houses as big as hotels would forget to pick up their children from the center. Their serial marriages resulted in several sets of parents and grandparents. I thought how miserable these people were to have so many revolving relationships. How disruptive and confusing it must have been to the children. I never thought about my marriage's effect on my children.

I kept very busy, keeping house, being a mother, and working at the day-care center. One day I woke up and realized I had turned from an angry young girl into a blind wife and mother who had no eyes or time but for her children. My mate was following his family script—living his own life, disappearing on the weekends, indulging his love of new cars, carousing with fast women, and using our family's money to do so.

We had just purchased a canary-yellow Mustang. It was 1970 and the Vietnam War was raging. Three Dog Night's "Mama Told Me Not to Come" was a super popular song that year. One Saturday night José and I had planned to go to a wedding. I got dressed while José went out to gas up the car. I had a babysitter lined up, and I waited and waited and waited. Ten o'clock came, midnight came, and two o'clock passed. I paced and paced and looked outside the window. At 4:45 A.M., I heard the door open and José tiptoe into the apartment. He had forgotten something and grabbed the item and was on his way back to the car when I hurried after him as I wrapped my chenille robe around me. He quickly packed himself into the car populated with at least four women. He must have told one of them that I was his mother because I heard one of them say, "Hey, listen to your mother because she is calling you." He peeled out of the parking space and left me on the sidewalk muttering to myself.

My frustration and anger built as I waited for José's return. I stewed and fumed. I'm not sure what angered me the most about José: the floozies or his telling them I was his mother. I do remember, though, that it was zero-degree weather, so I let him into the apartment.

I thought to myself, "He thinks I'm his mother. Well, then, I'll treat him like a naughty little boy." José started to remove his tie, then his shirt, and finally his belt and pants. He seemed so smug and self-content, with a heavy dose of booze in his belly. I flew at him and backed him up to the apartment door. It was an easy matter to push him out into the cold in only his underwear. He raced from window to window waving his arms and begged for me to let him back in. The neighbors all came to their windows to see this spectacle. He finally took refuge with his older brother, who lived upstairs. A few days later, sick and weak with a bad case of bronchitis and a mild case of frostbite, José returned home, unchastened.

No, these setbacks didn't affect José. Big José continued to behave in the same old ways, contrary to his promise to me back in Calexico: "I'll change." He could not change any more than a tiger could change his stripes. I took on more than my share of responsibility for his carousing. I then found how futile it was to try to control another person. I was beginning to change and it was not for the better. I wanted to return to my family so badly but I couldn't bring myself to do it a second time. I was becoming bitter and mean myself.

The Last Frontier

Unions were losing power in Chicago in the early Seventies, and the workers who earned fifteen dollars an hour had to take jobs for seven dollars an hour. The Trans-Alaska Pipeline was being built in Alaska. José and I followed his brother Gus to the Last Frontier. José became one of the more than twenty-one thousand people to get work connected to building the pipeline.

We arrived in Anchorage, where there was an extreme housing shortage. All we could do was crowd into a small three-room trailer, for which we paid an astounding nine hundred dollars a month. It was literally falling apart but it was the only housing available to us. Only two people could fit in the kitchen. The kids slept in the living room and we slept in the bedroom. We were packed into that apartment like sardines.

At that time, national news on television was a day old. The films were flown up by plane from the Lower 48. The *Today Show* was too early for us since we were four hours behind New York. We got only the *PTL Club*, with Tammy Faye and Jim Bakker. One shopping center was just being built to accommodate what was a modern-day Gold Rush. People would swing into town to purchase the clothes they'd need for the subzero conditions. Long underwear and bunny boots sold faster than business suits.

Unlike in Chicago, though, people were friendly and honest. In Anchorage, you could leave your purse unattended in your shopping cart and it would be untouched when you returned. Tourism was prospering, too. People were always selling others on Alaska. The place was wide open to all. Doctors lived next door to construction workers. Society wasn't layered in as strict a way as in other, more established places. Businesspeople wore flanneled shirts instead of business suits. Restaurants were filled with people whose dress ranged from Carhartts to cocktail dresses.

José, as a general laborer, did a little of every kind of construction work on the pipeline and put in fifteen-hour days. He stayed out of town many months without a break. We would follow him whenever we could—from Glenallen to Valdez. We were able to stay in Valdez for the last four years of the pipeline construction. There, where the kids started school, we rented a nice apartment. I, though, was unprepared for the snow—at least twelve feet per year. When the snow was shoveled off the roofs, it was piled even higher. People would literally tunnel through the caves of snow to shop at the two stores in town. It, though, was a beautiful place, surrounded by tall peaks and mountains. In the spring, wildflowers blanketed the Thompson Pass.

During those years José made lots of money. While working in the camps, he saved his money, at least at the beginning, and we, his family, actually saw a part of it. Alaska had its dark side, too. Prostitutes set up shop to service the large number of men who searched for fortune. Street drugs came with the easy money. Marijuana was decriminalized and very available. The city fathers closed their eyes to the plethora of active gambling operations.

True to form, Big José chose the lowest common denominator. As time wore on, he indulged in gambling, alcohol, and street drugs. For José, money bought access to more bad habits and excesses. He invested in foolish opportunities that went nowhere. A parade of loose women entered his life. Our lives became hell, and once again I was taught that there was no safe place.

He attracted unsavory friends—a troop of amigos who followed him around as closely as had his little daughter when she first learned to walk. How stupid I was to not see I married a replica of my father, Fidencio. José was also a carbon copy of his father, the demanding and inconsiderate Don Adolfo. The more he earned, the more he spent. He had grandiose ideas and made unrealistic plans. He figured he was entitled to things immediately without following the rules or going through the basic steps to get them. He thrilled at the prospect of risk. He believed he was smarter than everyone else. He was attracted to criminal activities.

In the early Eighties those who came up to construct the pipeline left Alaska. We moved back to Anchorage and purchased a duplex. Then, the price of oil plummeted. Unemployment was high. Alaska suffered hard times and the price of houses dropped sharply. People could not give their houses away. The banks would take them back and sell them for half of what the people who forfeited them had paid. Between the economy and José's self-indulgence and drug habit, we were broke and lost to foreclosure a fourplex in which we had invested.

Beauty School

~

Times were hard, and I needed a skill to find a good job. I knew that dental assisting was not for me. I knew that child-care work wouldn't put food on the table. The airport catering company where I worked was closing its doors. I knew there was no factory work in Anchorage.

I then remembered how much I enjoyed my work styling wigs in East L.A. in the late Sixties. My thoughts returned to the fun I had, as a young teenager, chaperoning my sister Mary to beauty school. I sat there watching her wash, cut, and perm the ladies' hair. I'd see her release each bobby pin and comb out their styles. I'd watch her tease her patrons' hair into a bubble or wrap it into a tall beehive. The worst part, though, was taking down those beehive hair-dos that had been lacquered in place for up to three weeks. There was no telling what you'd find in there.

To complete my beauty school training took a whole year of eight- or nine-hour days. I was a fast learner, and the time flew by, even with the pressures of studying and working so hard while caring for a young family. I'd come home bushed after a day of standing, but energized from doing what I loved to do.

My first job was in a salon located in a grocery store. Although I would never have imagined working in a shop like this, it was close to my children's school. It was important to me that they could get ahold of me if they needed to. I can remember hanging my license above my avocado green workstation that exciting first day on the job. Gold satiny wallpaper with a snake print lined the shop. In that windowless beauty shop there was more natural light than when all the blinds were lifted at my house. Despite my dark physical surroundings, I caught a glimpse into a saner world.

The contrast between home and work was like night and day. I'd go to the shop and the customers would tell me I was beautiful and talented. They were so thankful for what I did for them. I'd return home, on top of the world about my day. Then, I'd descend into the darkness with José's putdowns: "*Nunca vas a hacer nada*" ("You'll never amount to anything") or "*Eres una estúpida*" ("You are stupid"). When I wanted him to take me out, he would sarcastically reply, "*¿Cómo te voy a llevar? Mira que fea estás.*" ("How am I going to take you? Look how ugly you are.")

I referred to my customers as my "miracles" because their compliments were so out of the ordinary for me. Here I was, serving them, and yet they treated me better than the man for whom I left my family in Calexico. They enjoyed my conversations, my opinions, and my humor. They appreciated me just the way I was, and they liked what I did for them. I was suspicious of anybody who would be nice to me. I figured they might be trying to avoid paying me tips until I realized that my customers complimented me *and* paid me tips, too. Many of my customers became regulars, and they would refer their friends to me. One day, it dawned on me that my customers were not "miracles" but just nice people. This was the way people outside my home treated each other. This was the way most other people lived.

During this time, I began to read self-help books my clients would tell me about. I returned from a day of work and found José washing his hands at the kitchen sink. I couldn't wait to share with him my epiphany—that we could have a better life together. I said to José, "Grow with me because I'm ready to grow. If you don't grow with me, I will leave you behind. I see us drifting apart."

José dismissed me with a wave of his hand as he muttered darkly: "You'll never divorce me. You are too Catholic."

Life was so easy at the shop. There it was peaceful and positive. There, I was somebody and I felt good about myself.

I enjoyed the exposure to new ideas and reveled in looking at things differently through my customers' eyes. For the first time, I felt competent and professional. I realized that I had skills not only with hair, but with people, too. Gradually, the salon became more of a home to me than the house where I lived. I was wanted and needed there, not scorned and criticized. It was a safe place for my children to visit, and it offered me a way to support them financially.

And then I learned that my mother was dying.

Fly Free

~

In Amá's final days, I traveled to the San Diego area, where she lived. I sought a piece of her—something I could hold onto when she was gone. As I walked into Amá's house, I saw no luxury, just the bare necessities: a used sofa, a wood table with its colorless chairs, and on the table only a clean handmade tablecloth, sparkling white, with embroidered red roses and bright yellow leaves. I felt anger rising as I saw how little she had to show for her years. There on a corner shelf, among the photos of all her many grandchildren, stood a little statue of a baseball player in his uniform.

I asked myself, what was the purpose of this lady? She had nothing. I could count her belongings on my two hands—a couple of towels, her house robe, a few nightgowns and slippers. I searched and searched for any remnants that told me she lived here, a sense of her, a lingering smell on her rosary beads, anything that I could find that was hers. Any hope of a familiar scent was clouded by the overpowering presence of Pine-Sol.

I closed the door behind me and left for the hospital. In the waiting room, when I saw all of her children, nieces, nephews, grandkids, and friends, reality hit me like the spirit of the wind rushing by. I realized the reason why this seventy-three-year-old woman had nothing in her home was that she had already given it all away to her children—these being her greatest treasures.

Here we were alone in this hospital room, Amá and I. As I looked at her, I realized I blamed her for the anger I carried in me and that very soon, I would not be able to blame her any longer. I had never hugged my mother because I was afraid of getting close to her. What years I had wasted in anger, not knowing why.

As I sat beside her still body and the purring machine that sustained her, I wondered silently: "Will you be able to see us up there? Can you feel our hearts and know what's on our minds? This is my hope—that you will know my regret for not having shared these thoughts with you in life. Your life is finished and mine is left incomplete with your passing."

At her bedside, I lamented, "Amá, what a tragedy that I came so late to understanding you. No longer will you be weighed down with the sorrow of this life. They have given you a hospital room with a big window, and through it I can see that the day is bright and clear. The sun gives warmth to your cold body. Birds talk to each other, flying from tree to tree. Life goes on in its many forms. People walk, run, laugh, and cry. Some sit under the palms reading quietly. A fountain forms a small rainforest as it shrouds the surrounding greenery in mist. All this means nothing to me at this moment. I will not cry, because I won't be able to stop."

In her hospital room, I tried to assure her she'd be remembered: "I have to believe that where you are going there is peace and justice for everyone. We who stay behind will miss you for the rest of our lives. Your face will be in the flowers you loved so much, and when any woman holds a child by the hand, she will remind me of you.

"Tomorrow we will remove the life support machine and you will be on your own. I am sorry I failed you during this lifetime. Is this the only way I am able to learn a lesson? Does it always have to be so hard?"

I realized the depth of her wisdom for the first time: "I see your tired face take on a new dimension, and your life as it really was. Amá, you taught me perseverance, endurance, and the value of education. I once thought your life was pointless, but now that I am a mother, I am able to see the results of your sacrifices. You told us, 'Educate your children so they won't suffer in life.' You saw us finish high school and your grandchildren finish college. You told us, 'Don't wait for something to happen. Do it yourself.' Amá, in each of our children we can see a part of you. And what gift were you given in return?"

I assured myself of my brother's ability to help her complete her passing: "Just as you started your journey to this country holding your baby Joe by his hand, so you will be holding Joe's hand when you decide it is your time to go."

Watching her, I knew what her doctors didn't: they would tell me that those baby tears that just dropped from her eyes and her deep sighs are just bodily reflexes. But I know that Amá can hear me because her heart was the strongest part of her. "Amá, this is the last time I will touch your face or see you in this world. I won't stay to see your body taken away. That is too final for me."

At her funeral, the mariachi band was there as she requested, and played as she was buried. Her farewell songs were the ones she heard as a child on her little ranch. I imagine her soul transformed into a white dove, flying for one last time to her *ranchito. "Solo muerto regreso a mi pueblito,"* she would say. ("Only in death will I return to my little town.")

Yes, life is an enigma, a puzzle. Amá knew that until the day she died. She held on to that last piece, knowing that the hard knocks of life would in turn deliver to her children their own final missing pieces. I have often heard the question "If you had a choice, would you pick the same mother again?" Yes, I would!

To Amá I can quietly say, *"Adiós mi madre linda.* ('Good-bye my beautiful mother.') Thank you for giving me life. For this, I thank you eternally."

The Cycle

~

My mother's death changed a lot for me. It made me realize how short life is and how important it is to make the most of it. I had such an overflow of customers that I had outgrown the little beauty shop where I worked. It was time to open my own shop. Half a block from the grocery store where I worked, a new office building was constructed. I rented a space in it large enough for four styling stations. It was a corner shop with windows on two sides, so different than the dark environment at the other place. I decorated it in shades of pink and mauve. Alice's Hair Design was born.

To my amazement, "Alice's" thrived. I and three other stylists made the shop welcoming, like a home. We put customers first and offered them an experience beyond the haircut. We laughed and cried with them. We made sure we knew their names. We asked about their families. They were not treated as numbers but as friends.

While things were going well in my beauty shop, they were not going well at home. Often in the middle of the night, I would be awakened by the smell of smoke. José, falling down drunk again, would be burning whatever he was cooking for himself. I'd find him cooking a whole onion with a dozen eggs and tomatoes, mustard and ketchup spilled on the floor and smeared on the walls, while the burnt and smoking pan sat outside the window.

After José would be gone for a couple of days or weeks at a time, he would reemerge as if nothing had happened. He'd come home, take a shower, and open the refrigerator to eat whatever there was. Then, he went to bed like a king. He made no excuses or explanations for his absences. He would not bother to explain to someone so unimportant as he considered me. Slowly my marriage turned into a boxing match in which I was always the loser. I look back and wonder why I fought so hard to keep this worthless man in my life.

Unlike my mother, I did not just stand there and take it. Oh, no. I spent a lot of energy divining ways to get even. To cool José off from chasing other women, I washed his underwear in bleach and dried them without rinsing. The fabric burned him and caused him to walk like a cowboy for a few weeks. In short order he was back on his high horse. I ripped up his clothes and tore dollar bills into pieces to prove to him that I could be wasteful, too. I punched holes in the walls to vent my anger and hurt. I threw dishes at him and broke out his car windows. I didn't realize that these actions cost me more than they did him. They diminished me.

José would come home drunk and angry. He'd plant himself on the couch and displace the children who had been sitting there, watching their cartoons. With no regard for them, he'd change the channel and shoo them away. When he, loud and obnoxious, came home in the middle of the night, I'd implore him, "*José, por favor apláquete que los niños están dormiendo.*" ("José, please settle down, the children are sleeping.")

His scornful answer: "*A mí me importa una madre . . .*" ('I don't give a mother . . .') I'll do whatever I feel like." He'd show his authority by kicking the doors, breaking the windows, and throwing the plants. There was no use in calling the police. They'd tell me that it was his house too.

José was addicted to drugs and alcohol, but I was worse. I was addicted to chaos and anger. I was so focused on José that I abandoned my children. They were viewed as interruptions rather than the precious souls they were. They were left to raise themselves. They might as well have been on the streets of Mexico, where kids raised kids and never really grew up.

They huddled together, frightened of both of us, and I was too absorbed to even notice their plight. When José and I would begin to fight, my son would grab his little sister, and she would cling to him like an abandoned child. Her eyes were large with terror and his were narrowed with anger. I could hear my baby girl's voice in the background, calling out, "Stop! Pop, please stop!" My children were being victimized even as I had been. They were experiencing a replay of my own nightmares, the ripping apart of their own emotions. I, who hated that my mother forced us to endure such situations, was doing the same thing! Life was making me swallow the words I had spoken years ago, that I would never put anyone through what I had been through.

One day, though, Little José, then thirteen, gave me a wakeup call. His father had taken his week's earnings and once again disappeared for several days. After going through his own funds, José returned to pick up the family's checkbook. I was in the shower when he came. When my son told me about his father taking the checkbook, I grabbed my son by the neck and demanded that he tell me why he'd let that happen. I now can't imagine how I expected him to stand up to his father. I armed myself with a kitchen knife, got my keys, and commanded my son to get in the car. I started speeding down the road like a mad woman, looking out for my husband. I then heard a small voice in the backseat say, "Mom, you are going to kill us driving this way."

Little José calmly continued, "My dad doesn't get drunk because he wants to make you mad. He does it because he loves to drink. He will never look after us because he's too busy taking care of himself first." When this child spoke those words, it was as if the Holy Spirit had talked to me through him. I was so ashamed that my son had learned this lesson before I, as an adult, had. Out of the mouths of babes . . .

I suddenly realized the futility of giving in to the power of rage. Mine was a wrath so strong it made me lose all sense of balance about what was really important. My anger was like a beast, a grotesque creature with flames spewing from its mouth and fingers like daggers ready to slash anything in its path. I was turning my home into a carnival funhouse with crazy mirrors. The abnormal had become normal. Hate had been interpreted as love. This was not the life I wanted for my children or myself. Something had to change, and I knew it was up to me.

I WONDER WHAT gave me the courage to divorce Big José. Was it my grown children threatening not to come to Thanksgiving dinner if he was going to be there? Was it my mother's death? Was it writing the story of my mother's life that made me confront my own? Whatever, today I am free. I have come to believe that I am responsible for shaping my life. I can simply choose to rise above the hurts of the past and focus on the blessings that surround me—big and small. My children both rejected the life of abuse. They are happy, healthy, and successful. We have beaten the powerful forces of destruction that threatened to rob us of joy and power.